ORWELL'S ISLAND

George, Jura and 1984

Les Wilson

Saraband

Published by Saraband
3 Clairmont Gardens
Glasgow, G3 7LW
www.saraband.net

ISBN: 9781913393779
eISBN: 9781915089953

1 2 3 4 5 6 7 8 9 10

Printed and bound in Great Britain by Clays Ltd, Elcograf S.p.A.

MIX
Paper | Supporting
responsible forestry
FSC® C018072

Contents

For my daughters
Kate and Kirsty

I am glad to see you make a point of calling them
'Scotchmen', not 'Scotsmen' as they like to be called.
I find this a good easy way of annoying them.

George Orwell, Letter to Anthony Powell

Thinking always of my island in the Hebrides,
which I suppose I shall never possess or see.

George Orwell, Diaries

Illustrations

*Photographs marked * are © by the Blair family, reproduced here by courtesy of Richard Blair.*

Introduction

In the kitchen of a remote farmhouse in the Inner Hebrides, on a cold and windy January morning in 1950, the six familiar pips of the Greenwich Time Signal announced the eight o'clock news. Ricky Blair gave it the scant attention due from any active near six-year-old, but the radio broadcast shocked his Aunt Avril and Bill Dunn, the man who became Ricky's Uncle Bill: 'The death occurred in London today of Mr George Orwell, the author, at the age of forty-six. He had been ill for a long time ...'

The BBC Home Service had announced the death of Ricky's father, Eric Arthur Blair, the writer famed as George Orwell. Living too remotely to be contacted by telegram, and miles from the nearest telephone, it was the first news his family had of Orwell's death.

George Orwell's time on the island of Jura was short but deeply significant in the history of twentieth-century literature. His reputation as a great novelist rests, mainly, on just two works. In the second of these he crystallised a lifetime of astute observation, bitter experience and rigorous thought into one of the most important books of our age. Written in the era of Stalin's USSR, it remains chillingly relevant in our age of Putin's gangster/oligarch Russian regime and authoritarian challenges to Western democracies.

Barnhill farmhouse in the north of the sparsely populated island provided the seclusion that Orwell craved to write this serious work of literature, but Jura meant much more to him than a mere writer's retreat. In the words of his son, Richard Blair: 'This wasn't a holiday for us. Everything my dad wrote and said indicates that he wanted to be here full time. For him Jura was home.'

It was serendipity that brought Orwell to Jura to write *Nineteen Eighty-Four*. The offer of an empty house at a low rent, owned by a neighbour-of-a-friend, promised the newly famous author of *Animal Farm* the isolation he needed to finally write a novel that had been roiling away inside his head since the winter of 1942/43. That novel secured Orwell's reputation as the most influential and widely read serious writer of the twentieth century.

For a stubborn, self-reliant man used to roughing it, grasping the chance of a house 'at the end of a rough track' with the nearest telephone five miles away, was an easy decision. What is remarkable is that Orwell – who for most of his life nursed a deep dislike, even hatred, of Scots – considered living in Scotland at all, far less decided to settle there. The many friends who knew of Orwell's anti-Scottish prejudice could never have predicted that the dissident, but patriotic, Englishman would move to what he had dismissed as the land of 'burns, braes, kilts, sporrans, claymores, bagpipes and the like'. But Jura became the place where Orwell decided to put down roots. My own admiration for Orwell, along with curiosity about the roots of his long hostility to 'Scotchmen' (as he deliberately called them to give offence), and a desire to understand the benign influence of Jura and its people on the brilliant but crotchety English author, were the catalysts for this book.

An English son-of-the-empire and a product of his era and class, Orwell was not a man to keep his prejudices to himself. These were many and varied. He frequently denigrated homosexuals, calling them 'nancy boys' and 'pansies' (how he would have hated the appropriation of the word 'gay'). 'All tobacconists are fascists,' he proclaimed. 'Scratch the average pacifist,' he wrote with contempt, 'and you find a jingo.' He deplored English Catholics, who he thought pro-fascist, and had a curious dislike of 'bearded fruit-juice drinkers' and people who wore sandals. He pilloried vegetarians, 'escaped Quakers', birth

Introduction

control 'fanatics' and other assorted 'cranks'. And for most of his life he nursed a loathing for Scotsmen. While many biographies and memoirs have mentioned Orwell's curious prejudice against Scots, I believe than none – until now – have seriously explored the reasons for it, or how his relationship to Scotland swiftly evolved upon moving to Jura.

While 'all tobacconists are fascists' might have been a one-off dinner-table squib to perk up flagging conversation, his anti-Scottish prejudice was evident in his writing and conversations throughout most of his life. His Scotophobia extended to a dislike of his family's Celtic surname, Blair, and very early in his career he ditched it for the resolutely English-sounding name by which we know him best. Biographers suggested 'George Orwell' was a rather random choice of pen name, but I will argue that it was a deeply symbolic and significant one for the man who had become a committed English socialist.

As a Scot, and a devoted Orwell fan enriched by a lifelong exposure to the author's writing and wisdom, I have always found his Scotophobia odd, and have loved him despite it, ascribing it to irascible 'English eccentricity'. In any case, I feel that I and my fellow Scots are in good company with pacifists, vegetarians, gays, believers in birth control and even 'escaped Quakers', whatever they may be. In the era we live in, the tables have turned, and the 'cranks' can afford wry smiles at Orwell's own crankiness. Essentially, I was prepared to dump Orwell's dislike of Scots into the compartment of my brain labelled 'Doesn't Really Matter' until I began exploring the origins of this prejudice and looking closely at Orwell's life on Jura, the neighbouring island to Islay where I live. It seemed to me that as well as penning a great world book on Jura, Orwell also changed his opinions about Scotland and the Scots. Having largely ignored Scotland throughout his life, other than to denigrate its inhabitants, and displaying great ignorance of it, he began to write presciently and even sympathetically about it. I was astonished to discover that Orwell began to support the cause of Gaelic, the ancient Celtic language of Highland Scotland, and a tongue he had once thought worthy of the dustbin, or perhaps the Ministry of Truth's 'memory hole'. He went so far as to criticise the paucity and amateurishness of the BBC's radio broadcasts in Gaelic, which means that he must have listened to them on the very kitchen radio that eventually announced his death to his family. In one letter, I found an account of him gratefully pouring a generous dram for a lorry driver who had carefully negotiated the rough track to Orwell's remote home at Barnhill, without condemning the man as a whisky-sodden Scottish drunk; and in an essay for the socialist weekly newspaper *Tribune* I found him intelligently analysing how the neglect of Scotland by Westminster would inevitably fuel the cause of Scottish nationalism. That has turned out to be a prediction as perceptive as those about doublethink, the re-writing of history, fake news and Big Brother's surveillance society.

His own slave-owning ancestry, the landowning snobs of his early school days, and the racist boors swilling whisky in the 'whites only' clubs in Burma had poisoned the young Orwell's view of Scots and Scotland. But when Orwell first took the steamer *Locheil* from West Loch Tarbert on the Argyll mainland to Craighouse on Jura he made much more than a physical journey. He made an intellectual and empathetic voyage that forever changed his attitudes. Part One of this book describes Orwell's life and beliefs prior to his fateful first voyage across the Sound of Jura, while Part Two explores his life on Jura and beyond. It is a book about the accretion of prejudice, and the circumstances and intellectual effort that shed it. It has been written to enhance Orwell's reputation rather than detract from it.

Introduction

As Orwell wrote, gardened, fished, helped his farming neighbours and got to know the Diùraich, or natives of Jura, his attitude to Scots, Scotland and Gaelic changed. The time he spent on the island, and among ordinary working-class staff and fellow patients he met while being treated at Hairmyres Hospital in East Kilbride, confronted and overcame the Scotophobic wrath that he had nursed since his schooldays.

Jura, or at least the sense of community there, which allowed the farmers and fishermen to live their lives pretty much as they wanted while enjoying the cooperation and friendship of their neighbours, was perhaps what Orwell had been seeking most of his life. The poet Stephen Spender said of his friend: 'He was traditional in a way which goes back to a very old tradition in English life, before industrialization, to the English village. He believed essentially in small communities of neighbours who knew one another well and therefore he had a great deal of sympathy with the anarchists.'[1]

By all accounts Orwell was a good neighbour on Jura, with he and his sister Avril helping harvest his neighbour's hay and offering tea and scones (or something stronger) to locals who delivered his post or supplies. In September 1946 he wrote a letter to his anarchist friend George Woodcock thanking him for sending tea (strictly rationed at the time), as it would have to 'flow like water' when locals turned up to harvest the corn in front of his house.[2] His life on Jura among his 'small community of neighbours' sounds very much like what Stephen Spender believed him to be craving, except that he had to go to a Hebridean island rather than an English village to find it.

Orwell's writing life on Jura – where he also nourished a deep and loving relationship with his adopted son Richard – would have been impossible without the effort and care of his sister Avril Blair. It is argued that Orwell's marriage to the gifted Eileen

O'Shaughnessy deepened the writer's psychological insight and enriched his writing, but Avril deserves credit too. She was not a literary intellectual and did not directly influence the writing of *Nineteen Eighty-Four*, but she certainly facilitated it. Without Avril's efforts in Barnhill's kitchen and garden and her ministrations to the ailing author, her brother's masterpiece would never have been completed. I hope this book goes some way to recognising the part she played in Orwell and Richard Blair's lives.

For many admirers of Orwell, the beautiful and peaceful island where he wrote *Nineteen Eighty-Four* has become a place of pilgrimage. Those who travel there expecting insight into the nightmarish landscape of INGSOC's Airstrip One regime will be disappointed, but those wishing to pay tribute to – in the words of Christopher Hitchens – 'A man arguing all the time with his own prejudices and his own fears, his own bigotries, his own shortcomings, trying to argue himself in public out of these temptations' will find Jura a worthwhile and illuminating destination.[3]

Les Wilson, Port Charlotte, Isle of Islay,
June 2023

Part One

CHAPTER 1

He Thought 'Blair' Made Him Sound Scottish

'It was, then, with an impression of dislike, that I contemplated the first Scotchman I chanced to meet in society.'

—Frank Osbaldistone, narrator of Sir Walter Scott's
Rob Roy, 1817

George Orwell was born Eric Blair on 25 June 1903. Thirty years later, when his first book was published, the name on the cover was not the Norse/Celtic one he had been born with, but a resolutely English name. Whether deliberate or unconscious, his adoption of a robustly English persona chimes with what his friends and biographers have called his 'deplorable anti-Scottish prejudice', 'his hatred of them', his 'loathing for Scots' and his 'curious prejudice … more than whimsical'.[1]

The adoption of a pen name by the newly published author of *Down and Out in Paris and London* is commonly put down to the desire to save his family from being embarrassed by his writings about, and life amid, the low-life of two capital cities – at least, that's what he told his sister Avril in 1932. Orwell's friend Richard Rees, however, recalled that Orwell disliked the 'Scottish associations' of the plain surname he inherited from his father.[2] 'He was embarrassed by the name Blair; he thought it made him sound Scottish,' said his close friend David Astor of *The Observer*.[3] 'He disliked the idea of family origins in Scotland,' wrote fellow novelist Anthony Powell.[4]

In his 1936 novel *Keep the Aspidistra Flying*, Orwell has its central character ruminate disparagingly about his distinctly Scottish forename: '"Gordon Comstock" was a pretty bloody name, but then Gordon came from a pretty bloody family. The "Gordon" part of it was Scotch, of course. The prevalence of such names nowadays is merely a part of the Scotchification of England that has been going on these last fifty years. "Gordon", "Colin", "Malcolm", "Donald" – these are the gifts of Scotland to the world, along with golf, whisky, porridge, and the works of Barrie and Stevenson.'

Orwell biographer Richard Bradford describes the introverted and cynical Gordon Comstock as Orwell's 'twisted doppelganger' and maintains that the author wanted 'at least on the printed page, to detach himself from his past, some of which he despised'.[5] Author Jeffrey Meyers calls Gordon Comstock Orwell's 'satirical self-portrait' with many of Orwell's own resentments and complaints – one being about 'Scotchification'.[6]

Orwell's birth-name, Blair, was shackled to a not-so-distant legacy of Scottish imperialism, racism and slave-ownership. Blair is an ancient Scots Gaelic surname, originally a placename, derived from the word *blàr*, meaning 'plain', 'meadow', 'field' or even 'battlefield'. While a policeman in Burma, Orwell had many dealings with the disproportionately large Scottish community serving the empire there, and he found Scots arrogant, racist and whisky-sodden. Returning from Burma a fierce convert to the anti-imperialist cause, it must have been galling for Orwell to reflect that he sprang directly from slave-owning, empire-building Scottish stock.

Orwell's direct ancestor Charles Blair (1745–1802) was a wealthy slave master and plantation owner whose fortune eased his way into the aristocracy. Blair's ascent into the upper class was heralded in one of the largest (and at £200, most expensive) portraits by Sir Joshua Reynolds. Painted over five years and completed in 1766, it is more than two and a half metres high by three wide and depicts Henry Fane, a son of the Earl of Westmorland. To Fane's left sit, in what the New York Metropolitan Museum of Art describes as 'expressing carefully calibrated social hierarchies and emotional ties', the *nouveau riche* Charles Blair and Inigo Jones, a descendant of the architect. During the time it took Reynolds to complete the work, Blair's wealth had allowed him to court and marry Henry Fane's sister, Lady Mary, the Earl of Westmorland's second daughter. Wealthy, and now the son-in-law of an earl, Charles Blair had very much 'arrived'.

Charles's life was now in England, although the sugar plantations of Jamaica remained the taproot of his wealth. During his lifetime Jamaica had become the richest colony in the Caribbean, 'a Constant Mine, whence Britain draws prodigious riches'.[7]

From the 1670s the English, who had wrestled Jamaica from the Spanish, began using African slaves to cultivate sugar cane. As soon as they could – even before Scotland and England were united – Scots joined them in this hideous enterprise. The English colony welcomed skilled Scottish workers and in 1703 Jamaica exempted ships bringing thirty or more male indentured servants to the island from paying port charges. The historian and slave owner Edward Long noted: 'Many of the artificers who have come under these contracts, have settled afterwards in the island, and acquired very handsome fortunes, particularly the Scotch.' The 1707 union of parliaments then allowed Scotland's aristocrats and mercantile classes to join in the scramble and, whether artificers or aristocrats, the Scots thrived. It is believed that eventually one-third of planters on Jamaica were Scots.[8] The secret of a long and prosperous life on the island was, according to Long, avoiding the pox: 'It is probable, that the Scots and the Irish, who come over with sounder constitutions, less impaired perhaps by the scorbutic and venereal taints, are, for this reason, more healthy than the English; besides, the Scotch, in particular, if not more chaste, are at least in general more circumspect in their amours.'[9]

Acquiring land, and the slaves to work it, was another key to Scottish success. When the British government finally outlawed slavery and paid compensation to British slave owners, Scots – who made up ten per cent of Britain's population – were entitled to fifteen per cent of the money. Slower to get involved in the slave plantation business, the Scots had nevertheless overtaken the English at it. The slaves, who had been forcibly abducted from Africa or bred for profit in captivity, received no compensation whatsoever.

Orwell's ancestor Charles Blair, who had married into the aristocracy, was the third of his line to make his fortune through slavery. Edward Long noted that in 1699 the Westmorland parish of Jamaica was settled by 'the remnant of the Scotch Darien colony, who may now be traced by the names of several settlements hereabouts, as Culloden, Auchindowan, etc.'[10] One such Darien survivor was Colonel John Blair (1668–1728) – Orwell's great-great-great-great grandfather, described on a family gravestone as a surgeon.[11] Most of Darien's 2,500 Scots settlers had perished on their hellish isthmus, but Colonel Blair was one of the few hundred lucky ones to survive. Escaping to Jamaica, he thrived, was a successful planter, entered politics and in 1715 became Speaker of the island's House of Assembly. His son John increased the family acreage and fortune, and John's son Charles – who would quit Jamaica for England – inherited '150 acres of land in St Catherine, 930 acres in St Thomas-in-the-East, 500 acres in St Ann, 300 acres in Clarendon and 1020 acres in St Thomas-in-the-Vale, total 2900 acres ... Slave-ownership at probate: 392 of whom 211 were listed as male and 181 as female.'[12]

The wealth and prestige of Charles Blair and Lady Mary Fane's union had been long spent by 1857, the year Orwell's father, Richard Blair, was born, although the Blairs still enjoyed the trappings of class if not cash. Orwell characterised his family as 'lower-upper-middle class', meaning 'upper-middle class without money'. While the money sweated out of black slaves had evaporated by the time of Orwell's father, the social and cultural capital that it had purchased remained, keeping the once obscure Scottish Blairs within the ranks of the British imperial administrative class.[13]

Even several generations on, Orwell's Scottish origins were obvious. After his wife Eileen visited his parents in 1936, she wrote to a friend describing them as 'by origin Lowland Scottish & dull' but that one of the family had made 'a lot of money in slaves' although she goes on to describe Mr and Mrs Blair as 'quite penniless'. The descent of the Blairs into threadbare gentility was upcycled by Orwell into the fictitious family of the young poet Gordon Comstock in his novel *Keep the Aspidistra Flying*: 'The Comstocks belonged to the most dismal of all classes, the middle-middle class, the landless gentry. In their miserable poverty they had not even the snobbish consolation of regarding themselves as an "old" family fallen on evil days, for they were not an "old" family at all, merely one of those families which rose on the wave of Victorian prosperity and then sank again faster than the wave itself.'

As a young man with no land and no fortune, Orwell's father had to make his own way in some part of the world conveniently coloured imperial pink on the map. The eighteen-year-old set off on a career in British India's opium industry, a trade with its reputation mired in the exploitation of native labour, widespread addiction, smuggling and imperialist wars with China. Britain's insatiable thirst for China tea was financed by the sale of countless thousands of tons of opium to China – smuggled into the country despite the resistance of the Chinese government. Millions of Chinese were hooked on British India opium, and British India was hooked on the profit opium brought.[14]

Rudyard Kipling, who visited the kind of opium factory that Richard Blair worked in, described the production of 'the precious cakes that are to replenish the coffers of the Indian Government'.[15] By 1838 about 2,500 tons of opium was entering China every year, accounting for one-fifth of the entire revenue of British India. Meanwhile, opium exacted a terrible toll on the people of Assam who grew and manufactured it. In 1839, Scottish adventurer and tea pioneer Charles Bruce testified: 'That dreadful plague, which had depopulated this beautiful country, turned it into a land of wild beasts, with which it is overrun, and has degenerated the Assamese, from a fair race of people, to the most abject, servile, crafty, and demoralized race in India. This vile drug had kept, and does now keep, down the population …'[16]

Richard Blair's job in the Opium Department may have been a 'respectable' job in Britain's imperial hierarchy, but it was not an honourable one. The year after he retired, opium exports to China were finally banned.

Posted over the years to many opium factories in Bengal and what is now Uttar Pradesh, Richard Blair would ride forth for days on end to supervise poppy growers while slowly working his way up Britain's narco-hierarchy to become a Sub-Deputy Opium Agent (fourth grade) and acquiring a wife and three children along the way. Richard's bride was Ida Limouzin, eighteen years his junior and the half-French, half-English daughter of a success-ful trading family in Burma.

*

Eric Arthur Blair, a boy between two girls, was born in 1903 at Motihari in the north-east Indian state of Bihar. He was preceded by Marjorie five years earlier and followed by Avril, who was born in England, five years later. Orwell's birth coincided with the hightide of empire. Jan Morris, author of the *Pax Britannica* trilogy, cites the imperial apogee as Queen Victoria's Diamond Jubilee in 1897, just six years before Orwell's birth. Other writers suggest 1920 as the high point – the year when the empire had grown to cover a quarter of the planet's surface and rule 412 million people. But whatever year the empire reached its zenith, its heyday nurtured in Eric Arthur Blair a child who would grow from being a self-confessed 'odious little snob' into one of its most relentless critics.

The year after Eric's birth, Ida moved from India with her two children to Henley-on-Thames in Oxfordshire. From the very beginning of his life, Eric suffered from chest complaints, a fact that might explain Ida's move to England, leaving her husband Richard to the rigours of life in the East. When Eric was just two years old, his mother noted in her diary: 'Baby not at all well, so I sent for the doctor who said that he had bronchitis …' Orwell's lungs were his Achilles heel. Throughout his relatively short life he suffered from wheezing, coughs, pneumonia, bronchitis, lung haemorrhage and tuberculosis and – much against his stubborn nature – was hospitalised in England, Morocco, France, Germany and Scotland. Forty-five-years after that early childhood bout of bronchitis, while writing *Nineteen Eighty-Four* on Jura, Orwell bequeathed Winston Smith his own ill-health: 'The next moment he was doubled up by a violent coughing fit which nearly always attacked him soon after waking up. It emptied his lungs so completely that he could only begin breathing again by lying on his back and taking a series of deep gasps.'

When he was seven, the little boy who would become George Orwell was grudgingly admitted into a posse of local lads led by neighbour Humphrey Dakin, who later married Orwell's sister Marjorie. Dakin's gang let Orwell trail along as they fished the Thames, and fishing would remain a lifelong passion of the writer's. As he died, alone in his room at the age of forty-six in London's

University College Hospital while waiting to be transferred to a Swiss sanatorium, his fishing rods lay propped in a corner ready to travel with him. Despite their shared pastime, Orwell and his brother-in-law never really hit it off, although the writer was fond of Humphrey and Marjorie's children. It was with two of them and his own son that Orwell narrowly escaped drowning in Jura's notorious Gulf of *Corryvreckan*.

For eight years after Ida Blair's move from India to England in 1904, she and her husband lived separate lives with only a single conjugal visit from Richard when Eric was four, during which Avril, his younger sister, was conceived. Eric did not see his father again until 1911 when he was eight years old and about to leave home for prep school, ensuring that father and son remained strangers. Richard Blair came home after serving thirty-six years in India to retire on a £438 10s annual pension, which was totally inadequate to give his son the 'good school' education that 'the right sort of people' felt their due. But Ida was determined: one way or another, the son of a family with even threadbare, patched-at-the-elbows notions of being upper class would get his rightful public-school education and the status that came with it. 'I was born into what you might describe as the lower-upper-middle class. The upper-middle class, which had its heyday in the eighties and nineties, with Kipling as its poet laureate, was a sort of mound of wreckage left behind when the tide of Victorian prosperity receded.'[17]

Ida had identified St Cyprian's, in the comfortable south-coast resort of Eastbourne in Sussex, as a prep school which accepted reduced fees for educating bright boys who would repay the school by winning scholarships to Eton, Harrow or Winchester, thus burnishing its academic reputation in the eyes of the wealthier parents who could then be charged hefty fees. A number of these wealthier parents were Scots and, despite being almost as far from Scotland as it is possible to be on the British mainland, St Cyprian's fostered an odd cult of Scottishness. Owned and run by Lewis Vaughan Wilkes and his wife Cicely, the school counted itself a success, having crammed a fair number of its pupils to win places in top schools. Ida, while her husband was still in India, travelled to Eastbourne and convinced the Wilkes to admit Eric at £90 a year, half the usual fees. The eight-year-old thus donned the green shirt with pale blue collar, corduroy breeches and cap bearing a light blue Maltese Cross that was the uniform of St Cyprian's and began life in the school's privacy-free shared dormitories. The Wilkes had made a good choice – young master Blair did well, academically, at their school and went on to win an Eton scholarship. But while Orwell was bright enough to ease the financial burden on his parents, he was not thick-skinned enough to shrug off the recognition by much better-off boys that he was from a relatively poor home. 'There were a few underlings like myself, the sons of clergyman, Indian civil servants, struggling widows and the like. These poorer ones were discouraged from going in for "extras" such as shooting and carpentry, and were humiliated over clothes and petty possessions. I never, for instance, succeeded in getting a cricket bat of my own, because "Your parents wouldn't be able to afford it". This phrase pursued me throughout my schooldays.'[18]

Although Orwell was aware that his parents were poorer than most of his fellows, he and the other boys were unaware that he was on a scholarship, although Mr Wilkes revealed that embarrassing truth to him in his final year as exams approached, perhaps to goad him into greater effort. Orwell later recalled the humiliation of his scholarship status in his novel *Keep the Aspidistra Flying*: 'Even at the third-rate schools to which Gordon was sent nearly all the boys were richer than himself. They soon found out his poverty, of course, and gave him hell because of it.

Probably the greatest cruelty one can inflict on a child is to send it to school among children richer than itself. A child conscious of poverty will suffer snobbish agonies such as a grown-up person can scarcely imagine.'

Eight-year-old Eric was also a bed wetter, and he was routinely humiliated and eventually beaten for it by the headmaster. A good student and bookish, he was an easy target for the less intellectual and rowdier boys who would 'mob' him. He took refuge in books, including *Gulliver's Travels* which, he admitted, 'I stole and furtively read the copy which was to be given me next day on my eighth birthday.'[19] Swift was a lifelong favourite writer of Orwell's, but it was as a miserable and spasmodically incontinent child that Orwell first viewed the world through the eyes of the great satirist. He himself would bring a satirical lens into razor-sharp focus thirty-three years later in *Animal Farm*.

For five years Eric suffered the pain and shame of St Cyprian's, and many years later Orwell wrote *Such, Such Were the Joys*, a damning account of it. Among the miseries inflicted on him was the cult of Scottishness imposed by Cicely Wilkes, whom the boys called 'Flip' on account of her floppy breasts. 'The school was pervaded by a curious cult of Scotland, which brought out the fundamental contradiction in our standard of values. Flip claimed Scottish ancestry, and she favoured the Scottish boys, encouraging them to wear kilts in their ancestral tartan instead of the school uniform, and even christened her youngest child by a Gaelic name.'

Orwell and his fellow pupils were encouraged to admire Scottish 'dourness' and military prowess, along with the accoutrements of kilts, claymores and bagpipes. Porridge, Protestantism and a cold climate were also much admired at St Cyprian's, although Orwell detected a rigid upper-class distinction that was the bedrock of Flip's Scottish obsession.

The real reason for the cult of Scotland was that only very rich people could spend their summers there. And the pretended belief in Scottish superiority was a cover for the bad conscience of the occupying English, who had pushed the Highland peasantry off their farms to make way for the deer forests, and then compensated them by turning them into servants. Flip's face always beamed with innocent snobbishness when she spoke of Scotland. Occasionally she even attempted a trace of Scottish accent. Scotland was a private paradise which a few initiates could talk about and make outsiders feel small.

'You going to Scotland this hols?'

'Rather! We go every year.'

'My pater's got three miles of river.'

'My pater's giving me a new gun for the twelfth. There's jolly good black game where we go. Get out, Smith! What are you listening for? You've never been to Scotland. I bet you don't know what a blackcock looks like.'

Following on this, imitations of the cry of a blackcock, of the roaring of a stag, of the accent of 'our ghillies', etc. etc. [20]

Nearly thirty years later, Orwell was still evoking Scotland as the exclusive playground of the fabulously wealthy. In *Coming Up for Air*, protagonist George Bowling laments the decline of fishing for the ordinary man and complains that 'millionaires go trout-fishing in private waters round Scotch hotels, a sort of snobbish game of catching hand-reared fish with artificial flies'.

In Cicely Wilkes's mind Scotland and snobbery were intertwined and St Cyprian's posh Scottish boys featured heavily among Flip's favourites. She encouraged them to wear kilts when the school trooped to church in Eastbourne on Sundays, and for an end-of-term entertainment had her daughter and four Scottish pupils dance while singing Harry Lauder's 'I Love a Lassie'. Cicely Wilkes most likely did have Scottish antecedents, her maiden name being Comyn, the name of the medieval aristocratic Highland family that rivalled Robert Bruce for the throne of Scotland – a lineage likely to have nurtured her fondness for the sons of Scottish toffs. Former pupils, including Gavin Maxwell (there a decade after Orwell) and Orwell's close school friend Cyril Connolly, have testified that snobbery was endemic at St Cyprian's, but public schools in 1911 England were not there to foster an egalitarian society but to educate only those 'that mattered' and who would go on to run the country and empire.

With only about seventy boys at St Cyprian's, each one was well known to Cicely Wilkes, who liked to be called 'Mum' by the boys. When biographers Peter Stansky and William Abrahams interviewed her – in a room decorated with many old-boy photographs affectionally inscribed to 'Mum' – she told them that on the day young Eric started school she found him alone and downcast, and so knelt to put a comforting arm around him. She felt him freeze at her embrace. 'He was not an affectionate little boy,' she told them. 'There was no warmth in him.'[21]

Other former pupils were less scathing about St Cyprian's than Orwell. Photographer Cecil Beaton, at school at the same time, found *Such, Such Were the Joys* 'hilariously funny – but exaggerated' and is not the only former pupil to suggest that Orwell was embellishing his alienation and misery. Biographers, however, have sympathised with Orwell's view: 'a pretty despicable place', concluded Bernard Crick. Being humiliated for bed wetting was 'an appalling experience' that Orwell remembered 'almost to the end of his life', claimed Peter Stansky and William Abrahams. Former pupil and golfing correspondent Henry Longhurst recalled that if you were in Cicely Wilkes's good books 'life could be bliss: if you weren't it was hell'. Advertising tycoon David Ogilvy, who entered the school eight years after Orwell, described Flip as 'satanic' and wrote that she played 'emotional cat-and-mouse against every boy in the school'. Gavin Maxwell begged his mother to take him away from the school, which she did.

The experience of St Cyprian's so rankled with Orwell throughout his life that he penned *Such, Such Were the Joys* not as a young writer hoping that a piece of miserabilist autobiography might earn him a few pounds and get him noticed, but as a mature and famous writer with the best-selling *Animal Farm* behind him. Orwell believed that 'a majority of middle-class boys have their minds permanently lamed' by prep schools like St Cyprian's, and he decided to give it both barrels in the essay, which he wrote on Jura in 1947 while struggling to complete *Nineteen Eighty-Four*. Bernard Crick suggests that the essay may have been written earlier, and that Orwell just revised it in 1947 before sending it to Cyril Connolly's magazine *Horizon*. Either way, Orwell decided that it was too libellous to be published and it did not appear until after his death and that of Cecily Wilkes in 1968.

Orwell's essay expresses a loathing for the snobbish, self-entitled sprogs of the imperial ruling class, and particularly those of the Scottish and Anglo-Scots elite. And while it does distinguish the Highland peasantry from the absentee toffs who lord it over them and the grouse moors, it is nevertheless a damning account of Scotland – doubtless rooted in the first impression of that country to enter Orwell's young mind.

How did this vivid impression, glimpsed through the cross-hairs of the sporting rifle-sights of aristocracy and privilege, mould Orwell's thoughts on Scotland and the Scots? If the Scots were being oppressed by the 'occupying English', could it be it was because they *were* a lesser race? 'You had better learn your place/ You're a low and servile race' sings Lady Phosphate to Lord Crask of Runcorn in John McGrath's seminal 1973 play *The Cheviot, the Stag and the Black, Black Oil*. If that was the case, did the servile

Scots deserve to be despised? Self-hating Scot Mark Renton, played by Ewan McGregor in the film *Trainspotting*, declared that it was 'shite' being Scottish: 'Some people hate the English. I don't. They're just wankers. We, on the other hand, are colonized by wankers. Can't even find a decent culture to be colonized by. We're ruled by effete assholes!'[22]

To the impressionable schoolboy with massive chips on both shoulders about money and class, the Scots seemed either insufferable aristocrats or a forelock-tugging, lumpen proletariat that displayed all the hopelessness and powerlessness of *Nineteen Eighty-Four*'s proles: 'Natural inferiors who must be kept in subjection, like animals ...' And so the young Eric Blair, born in India of embarrassingly Scottish descent on his father's side and half-French on his mother's, would self-consciously become a devout Englishman with a thoroughly English name and a superficially cynical, but deeply romantic, attachment to English tradition and landscape.

The St Cyprian's BOGOF gamble – buy one term of school fees, get one free – paid off. Young Master Blair won not one, but two scholarships – to Wellington College and Eton, and after a single term at Wellington became a King's Scholar at Eton in May 1917. King's Scholars made up just seventy out of more than a thousand pupils at Eton, often paid very low fees, but were selected for their minds, not the money their fathers possessed. Although Orwell recalled that he was an 'odious little snob' at this stage in his life, he was happier at Eton than he had been at St Cyprian's. He was taught by Aldous Huxley, helped write and publish magazines and took part enthusiastically in the Eton Wall Game. But academically, he took his foot off the pedal ('Resting on the oars', as biographer Bernard Crick names his chapter on Orwell at Eton). It has been suggested by biographers that due to his family's financial constraints, university entrance would only have been open to him with a scholarship, and his marks were simply not good enough. Orwell's Eton contemporary Christopher Hollis maintained, however, that a gifted Etonian like Orwell 'could have gone to Oxford or Cambridge without costing his father a penny'.[23] But while university might seem the obvious path for a young man with a love of literature, Orwell had endured rather than enjoyed his schools and may have recoiled at the prospect of once again being 'the poor boy' among the toffs.

In any case, Orwell had set his sight on living life. His Eton contemporary and close friend Steven Runciman, who would go on to Cambridge and become a distinguished historian of the Crusades, remembered that Orwell had a romantic notion of travelling east. And that's what he did. At six feet three inches, and with size twelve feet, the newly released gangly schoolboy decided to join Britain's Imperial Police. Not yet a rebel or a socialist, he was doing what he had been brought up to do – run part of the empire with all the entitlement and self-confidence of the public school-educated English upper-middle-class. But the part of the empire that Orwell was heading for was a distinctly Scottish one.

CHAPTER 2

The Dirty Work of Empire

'All over India there are Englishmen who secretly loathe the system of which they are part.'

—George Orwell, *Burmese Days*, 1934

Joining the Colonial Service and travelling east to serve the empire was an obvious choice for the son of an Anglo-Indian family like the Blairs. Orwell's grandfather, Thomas, had been a clergyman who had been ordained in Calcutta and served in India. His father had been a government Opium Agent in India, and his mother's family had been teak merchants in Burma, with a sister of Ida's still living there. And of course, in India – Burma was ruled as part of British India – the opportunity to play at being a gentleman at little cost made it a well-trodden path for the sons of threadbare gentility: 'Theoretically you knew how to wear your clothes and how to order a dinner, although in practice you could never afford to go to a decent tailor or a decent restaurant. Theoretically you knew how to shoot and ride, although in practice you had no horses to ride and not an inch of ground to shoot over. It was this that explained the attraction of India … for the lower-upper-middle class.'[1]

'It was almost as nice as being really rich, the way people lived in India,' thinks Elizabeth Lackersteen, a character in *Burmese Days*, the novel in which Orwell sought to atone for his pukka-sahib role in running the empire.

Orwell returned from Eton to his parents' house to swat for the Imperial Police entrance exams in which he came seventh out of twenty-six successful candidates, but – lacking lands, stables, grooms and horses – he came twenty-first out of the twenty-three who took the riding test. In October 1922 the nineteen-year-old Orwell sailed first-class to Rangoon. Orwell was joining Britain's four-century long history of exploitation that he would come to loathe. That month another tyranny was spawned. In Italy, Benito Mussolini led 30,000 Blackshirts into Rome and established Europe's first fascist dictatorship. A new species of totalitarianism was on the march.

Although Burma was not the most fashionable part of British India, it was Orwell's first choice of posting. He spent his first nine months at the Police Training Academy within the imposing Fort Dufferin in Mandalay, the red-walled, crenellated and moated citadel that had once housed the palace of the Burmese monarchy before the British deposed them. Training was under the eye of Clyne Stewart, the burly Aberdeenshire-born head of the school and a devout imperialist. Stewart was a formidable character who would become Chief of Police in Rangoon, and after the Japanese invasion of Burma in 1942 would make a remarkable trek to India where he would join Lord Mountbatten's South East Asia Command as an intelligence officer with the rank of colonel.

Burma, which had once vied with Britain for power over Assam in northern India, had been invaded three times by Britain and finally annexed in 1886. The country was rich in teak and oil, and ripe for exploitation. When Orwell arrived, he found that imperial exploitation dominated by Scots. The first timber-felling company had been founded by Scots in 1839, and the quality of Burma teak and its value to shipbuilding quickly made its owners rich. The Glasgow-owned Irrawaddy Flotilla Company was at its peak when Orwell was there, operating more than 600 river boats that carried more than 8 million passengers a year on paddle steamers around the country's waterways. 'Can't you 'ear their paddles chunkin' from Rangoon to Mandalay?' asked Kipling.[2] The boats were mostly built by Denny's shipyard in Dumbarton and often operated by Scottish skippers and engineers. The Burmah Oil Company – originally the Rangoon Oil Company and the parent company of BP – was also founded in Glasgow and by the First World War had become the empire's biggest supplier of oil. The North British Locomotive Company of Glasgow built most of Burma's steam engines, although the giant Scottish engineering company William Beardmore & Company got in on the act too. The port of Rangoon was linked to the mother country and the rest of the empire by shipping companies owned by the Campbeltown-born Sir William Mackinnon, who the historian Michael Fry suggests may claim to be 'the greatest Scottish tycoon of all time'.[3]

Rangoon, it was said, was like a commercial suburb of Glasgow during Orwell's time in Burma, and it had been a campaign by the traders of that city which had persuaded Scottish aristocrat Lord Dalhousie to annex Lower Burma in 1852, after the second of three wars with the Burmese. Burma must have seemed like a part of a Scottish empire – a Darien scheme that had prospered. Throughout Orwell's five years there, conversations in the clubs and chambers of commerce would have been dominated by the brogues of men and women from all over Scotland who had travelled east in search of their fortunes and to enjoy the privilege that their white skins gave them of lording it over the natives – while looting their land of resources.

After training, rookie police officers were ordered to the first of a series of postings where they would impose Britain's law. Orwell was joining an elite. The native police force was 13,000 strong – but led by a mere ninety British officers who bore the responsibility of policing a country of 13 million people. The British conquest of Burma was still within living memory and much of the population, goaded on by students and young Buddhist monks, did all they could to cause trouble for the foreign rulers.

The Dirty Work of Empire

Often barely in their early twenties, young police officers faced isolation, loneliness, the resentment of the general population, the responsibility of making native constables arrest and imprison their fellow Burmese and, as Orwell reports, witnessing hangings. Compared with the lives of his public-school contemporaries attending university (*Brideshead Revisited* is set around this time), Orwell carried a considerable weight of responsibility. Early on, perhaps to give himself an air of authority beyond his years, he affected a rather Hitlerian toothbrush-moustache, which at some point during his career in Burma evolved into the Clark Gable-style pencil moustache that he wore for the rest of his life. Writer Anthony Powell never plucked up courage to ask Orwell about it but thought that it was 'perhaps his last concession to dandyism that undoubtably lurked beneath the surface of his self-imposed austerity ...'.[4]

Financially, Orwell was comfortably off, earning at the age of nineteen the equivalent of his father's pension, and with the prospect of making double that and being able to live in a style appropriate to his class. Speaking English and French, and having studied Latin and Greek, he was quick to pick up Burmese and Hindustani, and attained a fluency in Burmese that impressed two young Englishmen who began their training at the same time as Orwell. Biographer Michael Shelden reveals that, contrary to popular belief, Orwell was a very effective police officer who wielded considerable authority. Had Orwell stuck with the service, he might well have been made a senior officer, only in time to be killed or imprisoned during the Japanese invasion of Burma in 1942.

Orwell was remembered by a colleague as 'pleasant to talk to, easy of manner'[5] but he was nevertheless seen as a loner, un-clubbable and preferring the company of books to that of the policemen, soldiers, oil men, marine engineers and planters who frequented the whites-only clubhouse bars and billiard rooms. But as Orwell performed his duties he also observed, remembered and reflected on what he and his countrymen were doing in Burma: 'I was in the police, which is to say that I was part of the actual machinery of despotism. Moreover, in the police you see the dirty work of Empire at close quarters, and there is an appreciable difference between doing dirty work and merely profiting by it.'[6]

Orwell biographer Richard Bradford likens Burma during Orwell's time there to 'an early twentieth-century version of a slave plantation'.[7] While the Burma police officers regularly toured remote villages to settle disputes between the natives, much of their work was the protection of British property in the face of a resentful and sometimes militant population. On his travels through Burma, Orwell would occasionally meet another member of the white tribe who was as ashamed as he was of the conduct of Britain's imperial adventure:

All over India there are Englishmen who secretly loathe the system of which they are part; and just occasionally, when they are quite certain of being in the right company, their hidden bitterness overflows. I remember a night I spent on the train with a man in the Educational Service, a stranger to myself whose name I never discovered. It was too hot to sleep and we spent the night in talking. Half an hour's cautious questioning decided each of us that the other was 'safe'; and then for hours, while the train jolted slowly through the pitch-black night, sitting up in our bunks with bottles of beer handy, we damned the British Empire – damned it from the inside, intelligently and intimately. It did us both good. But we had been speaking forbidden things, and in the haggard morning light when the train crawled into Mandalay, we parted as guiltily as any adulterous couple.[8]

Orwell might well have recalled this shared subversion while on Jura writing the scene in *Nineteen Eighty-Four* when Winston experiences what he believes to be a meeting of minds with the Inner Party official O'Brien:

> There was a fraction of a second when their eyes met, and for as long as it took to happen Winston knew – yes, he KNEW! – that O'Brien was thinking the same thing as himself. An unmistakable message had passed. It was as though their two minds had opened and the thoughts were flowing from one into the other through their eyes. 'I am with you,' O'Brien seemed to be saying to him. 'I know precisely what you are feeling. I know all about your contempt, your hatred, your disgust. But don't worry, I am on your side!' And then the flash of intelligence was gone, and O'Brien's face was as inscrutable as everybody else's.

Or perhaps Orwell was thinking of a memory of shared imperial scepticism when Julia tells Winston: 'It was something in your face. I thought I'd take a chance. I'm good at spotting people who don't belong. As soon as I saw you I knew you were against THEM.'

In an autobiographical note written in 1940 Orwell dates his first 'vague ideas' of becoming a writer to 1927 when he resigned from the Burma police: 'I gave it up partly because the climate had ruined my health, partly because I already had vague ideas about writing books, but mainly because I could not go on any longer serving an imperialism I had come to regard as very largely a racket.'[9]

But whatever his feelings about writing during his time in Burma, he was certainly absorbing experiences that would make him a writer of distinction. Two of his most famous essays reflect his years in the Burma police. *A Hanging*, published four years after he left Burma, describes the execution of a Burmese native:

It was about forty yards to the gallows. I watched the bare brown back of the prisoner marching in front of me. He walked clumsily with his bound arms, but quite steadily, with that bobbing gait of the Indian who never straightens his knees. At each step his muscles slid neatly into place, the lock of hair on his scalp danced up and down, his feet printed themselves on the wet gravel. And once, in spite of the men who gripped him by each shoulder, he stepped slightly aside to avoid a puddle on the path.

It is curious, but till that moment I had never realized what it means to destroy a healthy, conscious man. When I saw the prisoner step aside to avoid the puddle, I saw the mystery, the unspeakable wrongness, of cutting a life short when it is in full tide.

Shooting an Elephant, published almost a decade after his departure from Burma, not only tells of the killing of such a creature but is a powerful metaphor for British imperialism:

And it was at this moment, as I stood there with the rifle in my hands, that I first grasped the hollowness, the futility of the white man's dominion in the East. Here was I, the white man with his gun, standing in front of the unarmed native crowd – seemingly the leading actor of the piece; but in reality I was only an absurd puppet pushed to and fro by the will of those yellow faces behind. I perceived in this moment that when the white man turns tyrant it is his own freedom that he destroys.

Both these essays represent Orwell at his finest, although critics debate whether they are fact, fiction or something in between. In comparison, his novel *Burmese Days* is a relatively minor piece of literature, important for those interested in

Orwell's development from a minor to major writer, rather than as a stand-alone work of art. But although lacking the sureness of his two great Burma essays, *Burmese Days* works well on a polemic level – revealing the despotism, snobbery, sense of entitlement and racism of the white Brahmins. It is also a powerful reminder that the imperial masters were by no means all English. In *Burmese Days* Orwell has his teak planter protagonist John Flory draw attention to the over-representation of Scots around the empire: 'The British Empire is simply a device for giving trade monopolies to the English – or rather to gangs of Jews and Scotchmen.' Of course, you cannot attribute the beliefs or views of a fictitious character to his or her author, but in the light of Orwell's ingrained antagonism to Scots it is telling that he draws attention to the disproportionate number of Scots lording it over the natives in Britain's empire and in Burma in particular. Orwell's lifelong hostility to Scots may have been formed at St Cyprian's, but it was heavily reinforced by his experience of Scots planters, engineers, oil men and officials who had set themselves up as Burma's pukka-sahibs. Orwell skewers the type in *Burmese Days*. Two Scots appear in the book – both drunks, and at least one a racist.[10] One is described as 'an old Scotch gin-soaker' who says, when a white man removes his topi while passing a native funeral: 'Remember laddie, always remember, we are sahiblog and they are dirrt!' And there is a Glasgow electrician named Macdougall, 'sacked from the Irrawaddy Flotilla Company for drunkenness, and now making a precarious living out of a garage. Macdougall is a dull lout, only interested in whisky and magnetos.'

The ingrained racism of such men is illustrated in *Burmese Days* in a scene where a teak planter who is a stalwart of 'the club' berates a visiting white Military Police officer for kicking a servant:

'Who are YOU to come kicking our servants?'

'Bosh, my good chap. Needed kicking. You've let your servants get out of hand here.'

'You damned, insolent young tick, what's it got to do with YOU if he needed kicking? You're not even a member of this Club. It's our job to kick the servants, not yours.'

Orwell came to loathe such attitudes but ratting on the bad behaviour of Brits abroad was considered bad form during the zenith of empire. Orwell defended his novel from claims that he had 'let the side down', saying: 'Much of it is simply reporting what I have seen.' Publisher Victor Gollancz rejected *Burmese Days* because he was afraid that the author's former imperial colleagues would recognise themselves and sue, or that the India Office would suppress the book. Fortunately, American publisher Harper & Brothers was made of sterner stuff and released the work. Nobody sued, but Clyne Stewart, the daunting Scottish head of the Police Training Academy in Mandalay, threatened to horse-whip Orwell if he ever returned to Burma.

Burma taught Orwell to detest the despotism of empire, as it did Flory, the central character of *Burmese Days*:

Your whole life is a life of lies. Year after year you sit in Kipling-haunted little Clubs, whisky to right of you, Pink'un to left of you, listening and eagerly agreeing while Colonel Bodger develops his theory that these bloody Nationalists should be boiled in oil. You hear your Oriental friends called 'greasy little babus', and you admit, dutifully, that they ARE greasy little babus. You see louts fresh from school kicking grey-haired servants. The time comes when you burn with hatred of your own countrymen, when you long for a native rising to drown their Empire in blood. And in this there is nothing honourable, hardly even any sincerity. For, *au fond*, what do you care if the Indian Empire is a despotism, if Indians are bullied and exploited? You only care because the right of free speech is denied you. You are a creature of the despotism, a pukka sahib, tied tighter than a monk or a savage by an unbreakable system of tabus.

Writing as himself, Orwell says: 'I should expect to find that even in England many policemen, judges, prison warders, and the like are haunted by a secret horror of what they do. But in Burma it was a double oppression that we were committing. Not only were we hanging people and putting them in jail and so forth; we were doing it in the capacity of unwanted foreign invaders.'[11]

*

Being part of the machine of empire put Orwell firmly on the radical road. 'I was in the Indian Police five years, and by the end of that time I hated the imperialism I was serving with a bitterness which I probably cannot make clear.' Orwell had had enough. In September 1927, while home on leave to recover from what was probably mosquito-borne dengue fever and living at the family home in the Suffolk town of Southwold, Orwell penned his resignation. It was not a spur-of-the-moment decision:

When I came home on leave in 1927 I was already half determined to throw up my job, and one sniff of English air decided me. I was not going back to be a part of that evil despotism. But I wanted much more than merely to escape from my job. For five years I had been part of an oppressive system, and it had left me with a bad conscience. Innumerable remembered faces – faces of prisoners in the dock, of men waiting in the condemned cells, of subordinates I had bullied and aged peasants I had snubbed, of servants and coolies I had hit with my fist in moments of rage (nearly everyone does these things in the East, at any rate occasionally: Orientals can be very provoking) – haunted me intolerably. I was conscious of an immense weight of guilt that I had got to expiate. I suppose that sounds exaggerated; but if you do for five years a job that you thoroughly disapprove of, you will probably feel the same. I had reduced everything to the simple theory that the oppressed are always right and the oppressors are always wrong: a mistaken theory, but the natural result of being one of the oppressors yourself. I felt that I had got to escape not merely from imperialism but from every form of man's dominion over man. I wanted to submerge myself, to get right down among the oppressed, to be one of them and on their side against their tyrants.[12]

On Orwell's return to England, the Blair family had gone on holiday to Cornwall for September, and it was there that he told his mother of his decision to resign. His younger sister Avril recalled in 1960: 'Of course she was rather horrified, but he was quite determined that what he wanted to do was write, and he wasn't going to be any kind of charge on the family. He was determined to make his way, but he was going to do it his own way.'[13]

Joan Mullock, a Southwold neighbour of the Blair family, recalled that there was 'a bit of a row' between Richard Blair and his son as 'young men didn't give up jobs in those days. They did what their fathers wanted them to do, more or less.'[14] Orwell's friend Mabel Fierz thought that Orwell 'felt deeply' that his father looked upon him as 'a sort of failure'.[15]

Orwell resigned from a job that paid him a comfortable £660 annual salary, a considerable step up from his father's £438 10s pension. It would be fifteen years before he would make that kind of money again, working for the BBC. Orwell, however, had acquired a legacy. His five uncomfortable years as a uniformed instrument of imperialism gave him a visceral understanding of the first of the three great totalitarian 'isms'. An understanding of Stalinism and Nazism would follow, and all would shape the masterpiece he would write on Jura. Orwell, however, continued to take pleasure – albeit 'almost a shameful pleasure' – in Kipling's poetry, including *Mandalay* with its lines:

> For the wind is in the palm trees, and the temple bells they say,
> 'Come you back, you British soldier, come you back to Mandalay!'

These were the very lines that a mortified British ambassador to Myanmar had to interrupt Foreign Secretary Boris Johnson's recitation of while visiting the sacred Buddhist Shwedagon Pagoda. The ambassador hushed Johnson with a curt mutter of 'Not appropriate!' before he got to the lines:

> Bloomin' idol made o' mud
> Wot they called the Great Gawd Budd.

Once out of the military-style uniform of the Burma police, Orwell could dress as he pleased. He would soon develop his own uniform: tweedy suits or jackets worn with baggy corduroy trousers and blue workmen's shirts. It was a threadbare bohemian look that was imitated long after Orwell's death by many on the left who wished to be seen as having their minds on higher matters. But Orwell was very particular about the quality of his clothes and – from 1922 until 1949, when he sent for pyjamas from Jura – he bought made-to-measure clothes of the finest Hunt & Winterbotham's cloth from Southwold tailor Jack Wilkinson Denny. Jack Denny, however, lamented: 'He was one of these people who put on a suit and don't look well-dressed even when they put it on new. I never really saw him looking smart.'[16]

Orwell had returned to England the year after the General Strike in which 2 million industrial and transport workers had downed tools in support of miners desperate to resist wage cuts and worsening conditions. He soon left his parents' home and moved to London to begin his literary life, and to submerge himself among the oppressed. Tramping in England and dishwashing in France for two years gave him the material for *Down and Out in Paris and London*. In Paris, Orwell didn't plunge into the fashionable writer-in-exile set, and although he thought he once saw James Joyce (a writer he admired) sitting in *Les Deux Magots* he didn't approach hm.

In late 1929 he returned to his parents' home in Southwold, which was to remain his base for several years, although his sister Avril recalled that he loathed the place.[17] He tutored, had a spell as a schoolteacher and wrote, wrote, wrote. Magazines accepted some work and *Down and Out in Paris and London* was published in January 1933 with modest success. Compton Mackenzie told *Daily Mail* readers that the book was 'written with so much artistic force that, in spite of the squalor and degradation thus unfolded, the result is curiously beautiful ...' and compared Orwell's horrific account of a casual ward to 'some scenes of inexplicable misery in Dante'. The review – albeit from a Scot – must have cheered the author as he worked on his next book, the novel *Burmese Days*. Orwell was on course to becoming a fixture of the London literati; a new writer with a new name. He made friends, met girls and had even begun to think about the kind of girl he would like to marry. He was making the life he wanted, but only days after Mackenzie's glowing review of *Down and Out in Paris and London*, Adolf Hitler seized power in Germany.

CHAPTER 3

The Kind of Girl I Want to Marry

'You are such a dear old ass! I can't help loving you.'

—Rosemary to Gordon Comstock in George Orwell's
Keep the Aspidistra Flying, 1936

Down and Out in Paris and London – by George Orwell. With the publication of that first book, the author had finally killed off the little-known essayist Eric Blair. The writer chose that pen name from a short-list of four, expressing – biographers record – a slight preference for George Orwell. In doing so he opted for a solid down-to-earth English name, suitable for the plain-speaking English writer that he aimed to be. Georges are dependable: England's patron saint is one, and the king at the time was the fifth of that name. Orwell is the name of a river in Suffolk. George Orwell is therefore a very English name, apt for a very English writer. He told his friend Tosco Fyvel that he had never liked the forename Eric because of its associations with Norse heroes. Orwell told Rayner Heppenstall: 'It took me nearly thirty years to work off the effects of being called Eric.' Heppenstall, whose wife was Welsh, had just become a father when Orwell shared his dislike of his own first name and warned him: 'Don't afflict the poor little brat with a Celtic sort of name that nobody knows how to spell. She'll grow up to be psychic or something. People always grow up like their names.'[1]

To one critic, Orwell's rejection of his Norse/Celtic name was 'more than whimsical', but 'too slight a thing to bear the weight of involved interpretation'.[2] Others thought: 'Seldom can a man have shed one identity and taken another with less concern as to who he was finally to be.'[3] But can the choice of the name George

Orwell really have been the result of just a *slight* preference? Wouldn't a dedicated wordsmith like Orwell not have thought deeply about how he would be known to his readers? Authors carefully choose the names of their fictional characters, and it is reasonable to suppose that any writer would be just as careful over his own *nom de plume*. If 'Orwell' was only a slight preference over other possibilities it was an uncannily appropriate choice for a socialist. The twelve-mile-long tidal River Orwell is unique in Britain in that its rights of navigation, trade and commerce are owned by a town, not by the Crown Estate: the people of Ipswich, not the monarch. The River Orwell is therefore a fitting metaphor for the England that Orwell desired.

It seems clear that Orwell was attempting to change his kismet or karma when he changed his authorial name – and disassociate himself from his Scottish great-great grandfather Blair's Jamaican slave plantations and other taints of imperial Scottishness. And although he never changed his name formally – he said going to a solicitor to do so 'puts me off' – he used his adopted English moniker increasingly throughout his life when signing letters even to friends. Writer Julian Symons became friends with Orwell in the later years of the war. 'I'm not sure I even knew his name was Eric Blair,' he told the Canadian Broadcasting Corporation. 'You could divide his friends between those who like myself always called him George and knew him as George, and those older friends who knew him as Eric. I never heard anyone call him Eric, but there were obviously many people who did.'[4]

After interviewing more than seventy people who knew Orwell, the Canadian radio producer Stephen Wadhams concluded: 'For a man whose father was of Scottish descent and whose mother was half French, Orwell's rather aggressive "Englishness" was a remarkably enduring characteristic.'[5]

The Kind of Girl I Want to Marry

In October 1934 Orwell moved to London and took a job in a second-hand bookshop. He was determined to write a book a year, and for a while he succeeded: *Burmese Days* in '34, *A Clergyman's Daughter* in '35, *Keep the Aspidistra Flying* in '36, *The Road to Wigan Pier* in '37, *Homage to Catalonia* in '38 and *Coming Up for Air* in '39. Given that he was writing journalism as well, it was a remarkable output and a clear indication of Orwell's dedication to his craft.

Despite the treadmill of the typewriter, Orwell made friends, renewed old friendships and had girlfriends. At the mercy of prim-and-proper landladies, and unable to afford hotel rooms, Orwell took his girlfriends for *al fresco* sex in the countryside or even city parks. One, Eleanor Jaques, provided Orwell with a memory of 'your nice white body in the dark green moss', the echo of which we can clearly hear in Winston's forbidden lovemaking with Julia in a dappled, bluebell-strewn wood in *Nineteen Eighty-Four*. 'He pulled the overalls aside and studied her smooth white flank.'

Orwell's girlfriends have provided rich pickings for his biographers. One, tracked down by Bernard Crick, remembered that the young writer did not talk much about politics except to curse the empire and 'the Scots by whom he appeared to imagine it dominated'. Kay Ekevall, another girlfriend, remembered Orwell refusing to go to informal literary evenings given by the distinguished poet Edwin Muir and his novelist wife Willa (together renowned translators of Kafka) simply because they were Scottish.[6] Orwell would even cross the road to avoid passing the Muirs' door, such was his intense dislike of Scots. By all accounts, the Muirs were charming hosts and rather semi-detached as Scots, with Edwin a proud Orcadian who believed that his family's move from Orkney to Glasgow was a descent from Eden into Hell, and Willa of Shetland heritage. In the 1950s Orcadian writer George Mackay Brown found the Muirs 'kind and considerate' and an enormous support to him as a young writer, but Orwell would have nothing to do with the couple. Ekevall recalled: 'He had his own prejudices. Fearful prejudices. For example he claimed that all Scots people were like the whisky-swilling planters he'd met in Burma. Fearful prejudices, and he wouldn't take any argument about them.'[7] Despite this, Ekevall was really fond of Orwell. 'I just thought he was a nice guy,' she recalled. Orwell wrote to Eleanor Jaques saying that he loved *Macbeth*, and inviting her to a 1932 performance at the Old Vic. It was a generous offer, but a date that was unlikely to further endear him to Scots.

Rayner Heppenstall, then a struggling writer eight years younger than Orwell, was one of Orwell's two flat-mates in Kentish Town. Heppenstall found Orwell 'a nice old thing, kindly eccentric'. The three would talk over a lunch of bread, cheese and beer at a big table in Orwell's room where, 'Eric may have been inveighing against Scotchmen. The few Scottish nationalists then already vociferous were one of his favourite butts …' When Orwell became a literary editor and was commissioning book reviews, he told Heppenstall that he had sent 'the Scottish books to someone else (they didn't look much good)'.[8] Sadly, he didn't name them so posterity can't judge if it was literary quality or the Caledonian origin that put off Orwell from reviewing them himself.

Keep the Aspidistra Flying, Orwell's novel of idealistic young poet Gordon Comstock and his struggles in 1930s London, contains a couple of barbed remarks about Scots. Comstock, like Orwell, lived frugally on wages earned in a second-hand bookshop. Comstock's shop was owned by a Mr McKechnie, who 'wasn't a bad old stick. He was a Scotchman, of course, but Scottish is as Scottish does. At any rate he was reasonably free from avarice – his most distinctive trait seemed to be laziness.'

Later, Orwell has Gordon wonder if Mr McKechnie is really a secret drinker, 'in the traditional Scottish style'. Orwell's belief in the correlation between Scottishness and drunkenness is further revealed: 'Gordon went to the top of the Tottenham Court Road and took the tram. It was a penny cheaper than taking the bus. On the wooden seat upstairs he was wedged against a small dirty Scotchman who read the football finals and oozed beer.'

Like all writers, Orwell was influenced by what he read. Among his favourite authors was Jonathan Swift, who habitually savaged Catholics, Presbyterians and Scots. Enraged that Ireland was denied union with England when Scotland got it (1707), Swift denounced it:

> As if a man, in making posies,
> Should bundle thistles up with roses.

Swift predicted that the newly launched Anglo-Scottish ship of state was doomed to failure:

> So tossing faction will o'erwhelm
> Our crazy double-bottom's realm.

Swift denounced the Scots as 'a poor fierce Northern people' and went on: 'I defy any mortal to name one single advantage that England could ever expect from such a union.'[9] Queen Victoria, however, had loved Scotland to the point of making a cult of it that many Englishmen deplored.

When the Old Etonian novelist Anthony Powell sent Orwell a copy of his privately printed satirical poem *Caledonia: A Fragment*, Orwell replied saying that he liked it 'very much'. The little book, bound in Royal Stuart tartan, is a humorous but savage attack on Scots, their character, land, literature, music, art and infuriating tendency to turn up in England:

41

Alack! They ever stream through England's door
To batten on the Rich, and grind the Poor,
With furtive eye and eager, clutching hand
They pass like locusts through the Southern Land:
And line their purses with the yellow Gold,
Which, for each Scotsman, London's pavements hold,
And in return, no matter where you find 'em
They brag of Scotland, now left safe behind 'em.

The poem suggests a Trumpian solution to the Scots invasion:

Against the land of Porridge, Scones and Slate
Let us rebuild THE WALL, before too late …

Orwell replied to Powell: 'It is so rare nowadays to find anyone hitting back at the Scotch cult. I am glad to see you make a point of calling them "Scotchmen", not "Scotsmen" as they like to be called. I find this a good easy way of annoying them.'[10]

Perhaps deliberate misnaming is an Etonian schoolboy debating trope. In 2020 the Speaker of the House of Commons reprimanded Prime Minister Boris Johnson for repeatedly referring to the Scottish National Party as the Scottish 'Nationalist' Party. Such tactics still seem to work as Ian Blackford, the SNP leader in Westminster, was certainly irked. Johnson already had 'form' as a villifier of Scots and, as editor of *The Spectator*, had previously published a poem by staff writer James Michie:

The Scotch – what a verminous race!
Canny, pushy, chippy, they're all over the place …
Battening off us with false bonhomie,
Polluting our stock, undermining our economy.

Michie's poem also recommends refortifying Hadrian's Wall and suggests 'comprehensive extermination'. Satire? If the poem had been about Muslims or Jews, would the writer and editor have been prosecuted for hate crime? Does pointing out such stuff simply reveal that 'chippy' Scots have no sense of humour? Or does lumpy porridge at Eton instil a lifelong antipathy to Scotsmen?

*

Early in 1935 Eileen O'Shaughnessy went to a party thrown by a university classmate. Leaning on the fireplace were two literary types, George Orwell – a flat-mate of the party's hostess – and Richard Rees. The two had a lot in common: Rees was an Old Etonian and the son of a British India administrator. Although he was a baronet with a private income, he was a man of the left and dressed in the shabby gentility style that Orwell affected. The two close friends would both serve against fascism in the Spanish Civil War, and Rees would be a welcome guest of Orwell's at Barnhill on Jura.

Eileen's friend Lydia Jackson thought the pair 'unattractive ... faded and worn', but Eileen clearly thought differently.[11] She admitted to her friend Lettice Cooper that she was 'rather drunk, behaving my worst, very rowdy' that night. But Eileen had a playful, whimsical sense of humour, and the likelihood is that she was on tipsy-witty form rather than rowdy-drunken. She certainly impressed Orwell, who walked her to a bus stop when the party was over and returned to the flat announcing: 'Now that is the kind of girl I want to marry.'[12] He proposed within a couple of months.

Eileen was remembered by those who knew her as vivacious, slim and very pretty with near black hair and blue eyes. A friend wrote that her eyes danced 'like a kitten watching a dangling object'.[13] Eileen was unconventional, bordering on slightly eccentric, careless about clothes, haphazard about her hair but 'quite dazzling' when she dressed up. She was also highly intelligent and, with her degree in English from Oxford, far outstripped her suitor academically. While he had been settling village disputes and occasionally punching coolies in Burma, she had been studying Chaucer and being tutored in Anglo-Saxon by J.R.R. Tolkien. Eileen was widely read, held her own in literary conversation, and became the first person who would read and constructively criticise Orwell's work.

Eileen was born in 1905 in South Shields (although conceived in Lerwick on Shetland, where her customs officer father had been posted). She had an older brother Laurence, who was confusingly known as Eric, the same name as she would always call her husband. Despite being thought 'dreadfully untidy' she excelled at school, winning prizes and becoming head girl before going up to Oxford, where her failure to get a first-class degree bitterly disappointed her. Thus excluded from the chance of a top-flight academic career, she took over and ran a successful secretarial and typing bureau, a thriving sector in the pre-computer age. It gave her experience and skills that would be invaluable to her future husband. By the time Eileen met Orwell, she had developed an interest in child psychology and was studying for a master's degree in psychology at University College London.[14]

Why did this vivacious, attractive, intelligent and educated woman bury herself in a sleepy village and sacrifice her career to the service of her impecunious husband? She had clearly fallen in love with him, although she joked to Lydia Jackson: 'I told myself that when I was thirty, I would accept the first man who asked me to marry him. Well … I shall be thirty next year.' An employee of Eileen's 'didn't like the idea' of George as Eileen's husband, and Lydia Jackson thought that 'Eileen really should have someone much more suitable, more attractive, younger perhaps … George didn't look well even at that time.' Eileen's friend, psychologist Margaret Branch, said that Eileen had a 'streak of mystical dream' and that 'she caught George's dreams from him like measles'.

Eileen's untidy hair and good but unkempt clothes betrayed a rebellious streak unsuited to a conventional marriage, and Orwell's dream of a self-sufficient life close to nature where he would have the peace to write, became her dream too. In deciding to share a life without creature comforts with the impoverished minor author of three books, Eileen O'Shaughnessy's famous dancing eyes were wide open. Perhaps an insight into their relationship can be found in the novel Orwell was writing at the time, *Keep the Aspidistra Flying*. 'You are such a dear old ass! I can't help loving you,' Rosemary tells Gordon, the thinly disguised autobiographical Orwell of the book. It sounds very much like a line the writer could have heard from the mischievously witty but adoring Eileen.

As for Orwell, many critics agree that courting and marrying a highly intelligent and educated woman with a professional interest in the working of the mind changed – and improved – his work. Typing his manuscripts, she was immersed in his creative world, and it seems impossible that the opinions of such an intelligent person, steeped in English literature, would have been ignored by Orwell.

The pair were married in June 1936 in the village of Wallington in Hertfordshire, where Orwell had moved to write *The Road to Wigan Pier*. Although 'bohemian', the pair opted for a Church of England service in a gem of a flint-walled church – despite Orwell writing to a friend on the morning of his wedding about 'the obscenities of the wedding service'.[15]

There may have been an element of parental pacification about the church service, as the couple's mothers were both present, but the ceremony was also completely in line with Orwell's nostalgia for rural and traditional 'Englishness'. As Rayner Heppenstall observed, Orwell had '… a curious mind, satirically attached to everything traditionally English'. Eileen, however, introduced a note of rebellion and had the word 'obey' removed from her wedding vows, a radical gesture for 1936. Rosemary in *Keep the Aspidistra Flying* did the very same.

The cottage in Wallington was a place where Orwell could root himself in his idealised English countryside and where he could enjoy nature, and fish. He had a plot of land big enough for flowers, a vegetable garden and space to raise hens. He had kept animals at home as a boy and Roger Beadon, a fellow recruit to the Imperial Police in Burma, recalled visiting his house near Rangoon and finding it to be a shambles with 'goats, geese, ducks and all sorts of things floating about down stairs'.[16] Orwell found peace to write in Wallington, but a spare bedroom meant that the couple did not cut themselves off from friends who would come and stay. In love and newly married, Orwell was probably happier there than at any other time of his life.

For visitor Rayner Heppenstall, the couple's new home was 'not a pretty cottage' and the village it was in was 'desolate'. The three-century-old house was tiny, lacked both electricity and an inside toilet, leaked and had a tin roof, which must have made it like living inside a snare drum every time it rained. Into this were introduced furniture, silverware and family portraits inherited from more prosperous generations of the formerly slave-owning Blair family, along with some Burmese swords that Orwell had collected in his police days. The cottage had once been the village shop and, to eke out Orwell's meagre earnings, the couple ran it as such in a penny-sweet sort of manner. They rented a nearby plot where they kept goats for milking. Next to writing, Orwell loved gardening and the Tolstoyan ethos of literature and labour suited Orwell and was a useful preparation for the life he would lead on Jura a decade later.

Meanwhile, in Spain, a storm was about to burst.

CHAPTER 4

Spanish Crucible

'The world is a fine place and worth the fighting for and I hate very much to leave it.'

—Ernest Hemingway,
For Whom the Bell Tolls, 1940

George and Eileen's rural idyll ended on 17 July 1936, to be replaced by a nightmare in which George fell to a sniper's bullet and the young idealists were in danger of arrest, torture and likely execution. In Spain a right-wing military coup had been launched against the country's elected Popular Front, which was attempting to lead the country out of feudalism. The Italian fascist leader Benito Mussolini sent 50,000 troops to support the coup, and 'volunteers' from Hitler's Germany mysteriously managed to arrive in Spain equipped with tanks and Stuka dive-bombers.

Facing the fascists was an alliance of volunteer militias recruited from a patchwork of liberal, socialist and communist political parties and trade unions. They were joined by idealists from all over the world who, dismayed by the rise of Hitler and Mussolini, were determined to make a stand. 'It is probable that every anti-Fascist in Europe felt a thrill of hope. For here at last, apparently, was democracy standing up to Fascism,' wrote Orwell.[1] But in Britain, the Labour Party dragged its feet. Much of the Spanish left was anti-clerical and newspapers were quick to report that anarchists and Bolsheviks were persecuting priests and nuns. Labour – with strong roots in the Irish immigrant communities of Liverpool and the west of Scotland – dared not antagonise that left-wing, but small 'c' conservative, Catholic vote. If anything, Britain's Conservative government leaned on the side of Franco.

Orwell fumed: 'They have done the wrong thing with an unerring instinct ever since 1931. They helped Franco to overthrow the Spanish government, although anyone not an imbecile could have told them that a Fascist Spain would be hostile to England.'[2]

In December 1936 Orwell set out for Barcelona, determined to play his part in 'the struggle' – the name commonly given by the British left to the anti-fascist effort to defend the Spanish Republic. Orwell had gone to fight, not to write. For the already left-leaning Old Etonian, the Spanish Civil War was transformative – crystallising his belief in democratic socialism, enlisting him in opposition to tyranny from both the left and the right, and bestowing the insights that would be at the heart of his most significant novels, *Animal Farm* and *Nineteen Eighty-Four*, and his peerless first-hand account of the Spanish Civil War, *Homage to Catalonia*.

Seeking assistance in getting to Spain, Orwell visited Harry Pollitt, the General Secretary of the British Communist Party, who steered him towards the International Brigades, communist-led units of anti-fascist volunteers who came from all over the world. When Orwell expressed sympathy for anarchist units in Spain and said that he would make his choice of comrades to fight alongside once he had seen the situation over there for himself, Comrade Pollitt showed him the door.

Orwell turned to the Independent Labour Party and its General Secretary, Fenner Brockway. The ILP, a once-inspirational radical party that had been founded in 1893 by the Scottish trade unionist and politician Keir Hardie, was now a bit-part player in British socialism. It had allied itself to another minor party of the left, the POUM – the Partido Obrero de Unificación Marxista – a Trotskyist-leaning group that opposed Stalin yet had made common cause with other anti-coup d'état forces, including communists, as part of the Popular Front. Unlike other writers, Orwell did not go to Spain in search of copy. Brockway was adamant that he went to wield a rifle, not a pen. 'Oh, he intended to fight, there was no doubt about that. He saw it clearly as the beginning of a fascist conflict – Franco supported by Hitler, supported by Mussolini. I remember his saying that it would be an experience that would probably result in a book, but his idea in going was to take part in the struggle against Franco.'[3]

And so it was to the ILP office in Barcelona and its Tyneside organiser, John McNair, that Orwell reported late that month. He was immediately inspired by the revolutionary fervour of his new comrades in Barcelona, many of whom were Catalan workers or peasants. 'If there is hope, it lies in the proles,' Orwell, writing on Jura, would have Winston Smith declare in his diary.

The POUM was disappointed not to have Orwell simply serve the cause as 'a propaganda journalist', a role that Orwell may have seen as oxymoronic. In an article headlined 'British Author with the Militia', its English language publication reported Orwell's decision to fight, not write:

Comrade Blair came to Barcelona and said he wanted to be of some use to the workers' cause. In view of his literary abilities and intellectual attainments, it appeared that the most useful work he could do in Barcelona would be that of a propaganda journalist in constant communication with Socialist organs of opinion in Britain. He said: 'I have decided that I can be of more use to the workers as a fighter at the front.'[4]

Within days of enlisting, he was on his way from the POUM's Lenin barracks with a group of raw, mostly Catalan, recruits to the Saragossa section of the Aragon front. Orwell, who had bought a 'saloon rifle' designed for indoor target shooting when he was just ten, was competent with firearms. His Eton Officer Corps training – where a fellow pupil remembered him as a good shot – and Burma police experience made Orwell almost a seasoned veteran compared to his comrades, and John McNair even witnessed Orwell drilling them and explaining the rudiments of the rifle before they left for the front.

The POUM's bulletin reported: 'He spent exactly seven days in Barcelona and is now fighting with the Spanish comrades of the P.O.U.M. on the Aragon front. In a postcard which he sent us, he says: "When I have persuaded them to teach me something about the machine gun, I hope to be drafted to the front line trenches."'

Not long in the trenches, Orwell was transferred to a unit containing English volunteers assigned to the POUM's 3rd Regiment, Division Lenin, which was commanded by the charismatic and colourful Georges Kopp, a Russian-born Belgian citizen. Kopp would become a lifelong friend of Orwell's and marry a half-sister of Eileen's sister-in-law. The fighting on the Aragon front was sporadic and the chief enemies were boredom and the cold, which badly affected Orwell's bronchitis. He was, however, 'absolutely fearless', according to Bob Edwards, an ILP contingent commander. Edwards also recalled that Orwell had a phobia about rats. One night he fired at one with his gun, sparking off panic on both sides of the line and in the fusillade that followed his unit's cookhouse was destroyed. In *Homage to Catalonia*, Orwell wrote of waiting in a barn before an attack on the Fascist lines: 'The place was alive with rats. The filthy brutes came swarming out of the ground on every side. If there is one thing I hate more than another it is a rat running over me in the darkness.' Writing on Jura years later, Orwell would turn his rat phobia into a hideous instrument of torture in the Ministry of Truth's Room 101. 'In your case,' Winston Smith's tormentor tells him, 'the worst thing in the world happens to be rats.'

A number of spirited women travelled to Spain to join the struggle. One of them was Eileen Blair, Orwell's wife of just six months. Like her husband, Eileen approached the ILP to assist her passage, volunteering to be secretary to John McNair in Barcelona. With the help of Georges Kopp, she was even able to visit Orwell for three days at the front, bringing precious tea and cigars. 'You really are a wonderful wife,' he wrote. 'When I saw the cigars my heart melted away.'[5]

Orwell had one Scottish comrade of note in the ILP cadre of the POUM. Bob Smillie was a twenty-two-year-old chemistry student and the grandson of Robert Smillie, a miners' leader, a founding member of the ILP and an MP.[6] But however brave and gifted, Bob Smillie could not single-handedly challenge Orwell's anti-Scottish prejudice. While Orwell clearly liked and admired Smillie, it seems that the author granted the young Scot the status of 'honorary Englishman'. Orwell described the ILP contingent in his unit: 'The English were an exceptionally good crowd, both physically and mentally. Perhaps the best of the bunch was Bob Smillie ... physically he was one of the toughest people I have met. He was, I think, the only person I knew, English or Spanish, who went three months in the trenches without a day's illness.' To Orwell, the admirable Scot Smillie was the most admirable thing a man could be, English.

In late April 1937, after three and a half months on the Aragon front, a lice-infested Orwell returned to Barcelona. 'George is here on leave,' Eileen wrote to her brother. 'He arrived completely ragged, almost barefoot ...'

Buoyed up by the enthusiasm of the POUM members, Orwell was nonetheless critical of its doctrinaire politics and general disorganisation. The weakness of the Republican cause was that it could not field a united army of resistance but comprised a gallimaufry of militias representing different factions with different agendas. Orwell reached the conclusion that the communists, with the power and prestige of the Soviet Union behind them, had 'a definite practical policy' and 'were the only people who looked capable of winning the war'. His instinct was to follow the sound of gunfire, resign from the POUM and join the communist-led Brigadistas desperately defending Madrid. A communist friend urged him to do just that, and take some POUM comrades with him, but after 115 days in the trenches Orwell was determined to spend time with Eileen in Barcelona before going back to war.

Orwell was also in urgent need of new boots. For the habitu-ally scruffy author, hand-made boots were a matter of fighting fascism not following fashion. The writer had enormous feet and had difficulty finding shop-bought boots to fit him. Bob Edwards remembered Orwell as 'a big man, you know, with big boots, the biggest boots I'd ever seen'. Orwell was soldier enough to know that even the fittest man could be brought down by ill-fitting boots and, even if he had been content to leave his wife for the Madrid battle-field, he could not risk going until he was decently shod. Orwell approached a Catalan cobbler to hand-make him boots, but the job took more time than Orwell anticipated. It was, as Orwell recorded, 'the kind of detail that is always deciding one's destiny'.[7]

Had the cobbler got his boots ready and Orwell had gone as planned to join the communist Brigadistas – or if he had joined the International Brigades when he first arrived in Spain four months earlier – he would undoubtably have fought alongside working-class Scottish comrades, mainly trade unionists, socialists and communists who formed a disproportionate element of the British brigade members. Almost a quarter of the 2,400 men and women from Britain who joined the International Brigades were Scots, and Orwell would have been a comrade to many who would have espoused their beliefs and recounted their own lived experience of the idleness, depression and hunger of the 1930s in the gritty patois of Glasgow, Aberdeen, Fife and Dundee. When you recall the admiration Orwell had for the miners he met while researching *The Road to Wigan Pier* – 'The miner's job would be as much beyond my power as it would be to perform on a flying trapeze or to win the Grand National' – it is hard to believed that he would not have warmed to a socio-economic species of Scot he had not encountered at St Cyprian's school or among the white sahibs of Burma.

Orwell was never to fight shoulder to shoulder with the Fife miners and Glasgow shipyard workers who might have won his admiration during the desperate defence of Madrid. Delayed in Barcelona for want of decent boots, Orwell's life took a different and dramatic turn. Stranded in Barcelona, he and Eileen witnessed the collapse of solidarity as leftist forces battled among themselves instead of fighting the fascists. Orwell himself got dragged into the factional fighting and witnessed the demonising of the POUM as fascist collaborators by the communists. Spanish communists were ruthlessly controlled by Moscow through the work of up to 3,000 Soviet 'military advisers' – agents of the KGB's forerunner, the NKVD. Far from fighting alongside the communists in Madrid, Orwell would learn to distrust, and then to loathe them. He recalled: 'No one who was in Barcelona then, or for months later, will forget the horrible atmosphere produced by fear, suspicion, hatred, censored newspapers, crammed jails, enormous food queues, and prowling gangs of armed men.'[8]

Had Orwell's boots been ready in time, and he had joined the International Brigade, Bob Edwards doubts he would have survived. 'There was this murderous commissar, a Frenchman, who was political commissar for the whole of the International Brigade, and if anyone had criticism of the war effort, or had any "Trotskyite tendencies" – that's what they called them, if you were opposed to something that was being done you must be a Trotskyite – he'd have been court-martialed and shot.'[9] Leon

Trotsky, a former comrade of Lenin and Stalin who Stalin had assassinated, is the model for Emmanuel Goldstein, the traitorous enemy of INGSOC and Oceania in *Nineteen Eighty-Four.*

Orwell returned to the POUM trenches on the Aragon front where the six-foot-three Englishman stood tall amongst his comrades. Caught in a sniper's sight, a bullet from a high-velocity rifle hit him in the throat, missing an artery by a fraction. Against all expectations, Orwell pulled through and was eventually sent to recuperate at a POUM sanatorium outside Barcelona where Eileen was able to visit him. Medically discharged from his unit, his soldiering days were over – but his and Eileen's lives were still in grave danger. POUM members returning to Barcelona were being disarmed by the communists. The Soviets now controlled the Spanish Republic's formidable propaganda machine and their lies about the POUM being a fascist front were gaining traction. The pamphlet 'Trotskyism in the Service of Franco: A documented Record of TREACHERY by the P.O.U.M in SPAIN', by a correspondent of the French communist newspaper *L'Humanité*, was published internationally in 1938 in six languages. Shamefully, the international press lapped up such fake news and spread it like a virus around the world. The Communist mask was off, and everywhere anarchists and POUM members were denounced as collaborators and ruthlessly hunted down.

Richard Rees, in Spain to drive ambulances for the Republican side, met Eileen briefly in Barcelona, but was told by her that it was dangerous for him to be seen with her. Rees recalled that he found Eileen 'in what struck me as a very strange mental state. She seemed absent-minded, preoccupied and dazed.' At the time, Rees put it down to her being worried about her husband at the front, but later concluded: 'In reality, of course, as I realised afterwards, she was the first person in whom I had witnessed the symptoms of a human being living under political terror.'[10]

On 18 June 1937, two days after the Republican govern-ment declared the POUM illegal, Eileen's room in the Hotel Continental was searched, and her husband's notes and papers confiscated. One can only speculate if these might still lie deep in the archives of Russia's FSB, the successor agency to the NKVD and KGB. ILP volunteer Orwell was certainly known to the Soviet Secret Service, which reported on 7 July that he was 'the leading personality and most respected man in the contingent'. Historian James K. Hopkins, who examined available files, concluded: 'By labeling him as a Trotskyist, the Communists had in effect signed his death warrant if he remained in Spain ... Within a short time every follower of the POUM was either dead, in prison, or, like the wounded Orwell, on the run.'[11] The POUM leader, Andreu Nin, was arrested, brutally tortured and executed.

When Orwell turned up at Eileen's hotel, she hurried him out into the street to warn him of the purges. For a brief but anx-ious time, Orwell and Eileen were living in a secret police state – making Orwell among the most qualified authors in English to write about totalitarianism, and almost uniquely qualified to write about a totalitarianism of the left.

While attempting to return to Scotland for a pro-Republican speaking tour, Orwell's comrade Bob Smillie had been seized in Valencia by police under the control of the Communist Party and thrown into jail. There he was left to languish and die, possibly from peritonitis although suspicions ran high in the ILP that Smillie was murdered. Orwell was appalled by the news: 'Smillie's death is not a thing I can easily forgive. Here was this brave and gifted boy, who had thrown up his career at Glasgow University in order to come and fight against Fascism, and who, as I saw for myself, had done his job at the front with faultless courage and willingness; and all they could find to do with him was to fling him into jail and let him die like a neglected animal.'

Georges Kopp was also arrested and, although Orwell and Eileen risked being seized themselves, they visited Kopp and argued for his release. But they were unable to do anything except leave money to buy him food and cigarettes. Kopp was tortured and then imprisoned for eighteen brutal months, but he endured. The less physically robust and wounded Orwell was unlikely to have survived such an ordeal.

Hotels were closely monitored throughout this reign of terror and Orwell and Eileen slept rough until they could escape Spain. We now know that the NKVD had a file that denounced Orwell and his wife as 'pronounced Trotskyites', and ever since the publication of *The Road to Wigan Pier* Moscow had Orwell's name on a blacklist.[12] Arrest would have meant certain death as Trotskyist/fascist enemies of Stalin. The truth was that while Stalin was prepared to support the Spanish Republic with arms, he would not countenance the social revolution that Orwell, the POUM and other idealistic units demanded. Stalin foresaw that he would one day need allies against Hitler and would not allow a revolution on their doorstep to scare the war horses of France and Britain.

*

Spain transformed Orwell. From this point onwards his art was that of a political writer – a writer attuned to the lies and distortions of political debate. And while many writers, artists and intellectuals embraced Stalin's communism – before pleading naïveté and recanting later – Orwell had been Stalin-sceptic right from the start and would spend a decade denouncing communism. The writer Christopher Hitchens suggested that Orwell's impatience with those who claimed to have been duped by Stalinism is at the root of much anti-Orwell feeling then and now.[13] Journalist Peter Oborne argues that many on the left in the 1930s had a 'privileged relationship' with the truth that came from their belief that 'in a venal world, filled with vicious, unscrupulous right-wing enemies they are licensed to use falsehoods to secure their political ends'.[14]

Orwell himself reflected on how his experiences in Spain shaped his writing: 'Every line of serious work that I have written since 1936 has been written, directly or indirectly, *against* totalitarianism and *for* democratic socialism … what I have most wanted to do throughout the past ten years is to make political writing into an art. My starting point is always a feeling of partisanship, a sense of injustice.'[15]

The behaviour of the Soviet-led communist forces in Spain is at the very root of the coruscating satire *Animal Farm*. Orwell's earnings from that book then liberated him to seek out the isolation of Jura where, in *Nineteen Eighty-Four*, he denounced the totalitarian ideology that ruthlessly re-invented history, devised doublethink, denied the existence of objective truth and bamboozled the masses into believing that war is peace, freedom is slavery and ignorance is strength. If the Barcelona purges taught Orwell about politics, they also furnished him with the nightmare atmosphere of fear, paranoia and persecution that, twelve years later, he would pitch Winston Smith and Julia into on Airstrip One in the year 1984.

In Spain Orwell gained a profound insight – unique among twentieth-century novelists – into the nature of yet another crucial political 'ism' of that century. His Burmese experience gave him an understanding of imperialism, writing *The Road to Wigan Pier* sharpened his critique of capitalism, and while his service in Spain saw him fight fascism, it crucially revealed to him the horrors of Stalinist communism.

Returning to England, Orwell believed he had come home to a country that had failed democracy and given a free pass to fascists in Spain, but it was from the left that he found himself under attack. Harry Pollitt and others in the Communist Party were busy denouncing *The Road to Wigan Pier*, which had been published by the Left Book Club before Orwell left for Spain. Pollitt reviewed the book for *The Daily Worker*, condemning Orwell as 'a disillusioned little middle-class boy who, seeing through Imperialism, decided to discover what Socialism has to offer'. But while many Moscow-minded Marxists were suspicious about Orwell's adherence to the left, British Intelligence was not. Orwell had been under surveillance ever since he began work on *The Road to Wigan Pier* in 1936, and Special Branch continued to take an interest in him for the next twelve years, regularly opening his mail.

George and Eileen returned to the tiny, primitive cottage in Wallington where he began to write *Homage to Catalonia* while churning out reviews and articles, growing vegetables and keeping goats to eke out his precarious income. This division of time between desk and soil would become a feature of his life on Jura – whenever his health permitted him to work outdoors.

One day in March 1938 Orwell began haemorrhaging blood from his mouth. It had happened before, but it was the first time Eileen had witnessed it and she was profoundly shocked. She called her chest-specialist brother (a telephone had at last been installed in the cottage) who arranged for an ambulance and a place in a sanatorium where the bleeding was stopped, but he was diagnosed with tuberculosis and confined for six months. Eileen's biographer Sylvia Topp suggests that had it not been for Eileen's actions and connections, Orwell might have died that night.

A month after he was admitted to the sanatorium *Homage to Catalonia* was released – and flopped. Instead of hoped-for sales of 3,000 or 4,000, it sold fewer than 700 copies in six months. There were some favourable reviews (one from the radical Scottish writer Naomi Mitchison) but, with so many writers and journalists witnessing or participating in the Spanish Civil War, accounts of it were ten-a-penny. Furthermore, it was not an account that communist-leaning intellectuals wanted to read. In an essay about his friend Arthur Koestler (another anti-Stalinist who fought in Spain), Orwell reflected: 'The sin of nearly all leftwingers since 1933 onwards is that they have wanted to be anti-Fascist without being anti-totalitarian.'[16]

Today, *Homage to Catalonia* is the most read and admired account of that war in the English language. Given that Eileen too had survived the Stalinist terror in Barcelona and typed up, and no doubt absorbed, the NKVD-confiscated notes that Orwell had sent her from the front, one can only speculate what influence her impressions and memories had on Orwell's writing. Her husband's friend Richard Rees, who thought that a lack of interest in psychology and philosophy was Orwell's 'chief limitation', detected a striking change of mood in Orwell's work in *Homage to Catalonia*, in which Orwell really began to write about human beings other than himself. Sylvia Topp finds it 'amazing' that Rees did not look at the intelligent woman who was also in danger of arrest and execution in Spain and ascribe at least some of the improvement in Orwell's work to her. Furthermore, Eileen was studying for a master's degree in psychology when she met Orwell. What a resource for a writer to have a psychologist for a wife. What an opportunity to begin imagining the working of minds other than your own.

Orwell had escaped with Eileen from Spain to write a fine book. A Republican sniper had left the writer with a scar in his throat, but the scar was a scrape compared to the deep loathing for Stalinism that Orwell carried from the Barcelona street-fighting. Now he was to experience another dictator's war. In London.

CHAPTER 5

War, Uncle Joe and Comrade Napoleon

'Your Uncle Joe's a worker and a very decent chap …'

—Hamish Henderson, 'Ballad of the Taxi Driver's Cap',
published 1947.

In September 1938 Orwell left the sanatorium and sailed from England with Eileen to spend six months in the warm, dry climate of Morocco where he would write his most 'English' of novels, *Coming Up for Air*. While there, he took pains to observe and condemn imperialism in its French manifestation: 'There is one thing which every white man (and in this connection it doesn't matter twopence of he calls himself a Socialist) thinks when he sees a black army marching past. "How much longer can we go on kidding these people? How much longer before they turn their guns in the opposite direction?"'[1]

George and Eileen returned to England in March 1939 and *Coming Up for Air* was published three months later. The novel fuses nostalgia for the innocence of a bygone Edwardian age with a hostile critique of capitalism and the fear of a coming war. In one passage George Bowling and his wife Hilda attend a Left Book Club meeting where an anti-fascist speaker himself crosses the line into fanaticism:

> It was a voice that sounded as if it could go on for a fortnight without stopping. It's a ghastly thing, really, to have a sort of human barrel-organ shooting propaganda at you by the hour. The same thing over and over again. Hate, hate, hate. Let's all get together and have a good hate. Over and over.

It gives you the feeling that something has got inside your skull and is hammering down on your brain.

The capacity for propaganda to promote hate was clearly on Orwell's mind, and he would return to 'hate, hate, hate' – a full two minutes of it – in *Nineteen Eighty-Four*. Meanwhile, the conflict that the first-person narrator of *Coming Up for Air* feared was about to break out, and Orwell dreaded the likely devastating consequences for human freedom:

War! I started thinking about it again. It's coming soon, that's certain. But who's afraid of war? That's to say, who's afraid of the bombs and the machine-guns? 'You are,' you say. Yes, I am, and so's anybody who's ever seen them. But it isn't the war that matters, it's the after-war. The world we're going down into, the kind of hate-world, slogan-world. The coloured shirts, the barbed wire, the rubber truncheons. The secret cells where the electric light burns night and day, and the detectives watching you while you sleep. And the processions and the posters with enormous faces, and the crowds of a million people all cheering for the Leader till they deafen themselves into thinking that they really worship him, and all the time, underneath, they hate him so that they want to puke. It's all going to happen. Or isn't it? Some days I know it's impossible, other days I know it's inevitable.[2]

Orwell could connect Germany's grim torchlit march into Nazism with his own direct experience of tyranny, as experienced in Barcelona and British Burma. Through his relatively recently opened socialist eyes, he was now seeing his native land in a new light. 'We like to think of England as a democratic country, but our rule in India, for instance, is just as bad as German Fascism, though outwardly it may be less irritating. I do not see how one can oppose Fascism except by working for the overthrow of the capitalism, starting, of course, in one's own country. If one collaborates with a capitalist-imperialist government in a struggle 'against Fascism', i.e. against a rival imperialism, one is simply letting Fascism in the back door.'[3]

While the guns remained silent, advocating the overthrow of capitalism and refusing to collaborate in Britain's imperialist wars was all very well but, when Prime Minister Neville Chamberlain declared war on Nazi Germany, Orwell's English patriotism rekindled. Within days he had registered for war work and, although he wanted to fight, he knew his illness-wracked body would never again wear a uniform. He also nurtured a suspicion that lefties who had fought for the Spanish Republic were unwelcome in His Majesty's armed forces. The novelist Anthony Powell ('the only Tory I ever liked', according to Orwell) believed that being unable to take an active role in the fighting was 'a terrible blow' to Orwell.[4] Meanwhile, Eileen went to war, finding work in the government's Censorship Department in Whitehall, and leaving her husband alone in Wallington, except for weekends, where he fretted about his inability to play his part. 'I have so far completely failed to serve H.M government in any capacity, though I want to, because it seems to me that now we are in this bloody war we have got to win it & I would like to lend a hand.'[5]

Orwell was lonely at Wallington. He could dig for victory, but he missed Eileen and decided to join her in London. The move was a wrench and the last entry in his domestic diary of that period, dated 29 April, reveals what a countryman he had become: 'Planted out 1 doz. Largish lettuces ... let the tadpoles go, as not certain how many days I shall be away ... gave the grass a quick cut ... leeks are just showing ... some apple blossom showing ... 15 eggs.'

War, Uncle Joe and Comrade Napoleon

On May Day 1940 Orwell moved into a top-floor flat in Marylebone. He and Eileen sometimes spent weekends at Wallington but for the duration of the war London would be their home. A plan for a novel that had been coalescing in his mind since he had been in Spain was put on hold, as was a dream Orwell had of living and writing on an island in the Hebrides. Orwell first expressed that desire in his diary on 20 June 1940:

> Thinking always of my island in the Hebrides, which I suppose I shall never possess nor even see. Compton Mackenzie says even now most of the islands are uninhabited (there are 500 of them, only 10 per cent inhabited at normal times), and most have water and a little cultivable land, and goats will live on them. According to R.H., a woman who rented an island in the Hebrides in order to avoid air raids was the first air raid casualty of the war, the RAF dropping a bomb there by mistake. Good if true.[6,7]

No further insight into the author's dream of the Hebrides is offered, other than that tight, spare sentence in his diary, so typical of the author's writing style. But, given his situation at that time, the dream of an escape to the Hebrides was completely understandable, if fanciful. Just three weeks previously, in early June, a demoralised and defeated army of a third of a million men had been plucked from the beaches of Dunkirk, leaving behind their tanks, guns, equipment and 68,000 British comrades dead, missing or captured. The country's new Prime Minister, Winston Churchill, hailed the evacuation as 'a miracle of deliverance'. German High Command boasted of it as 'the greatest annihilation battle of all time'.

For Orwell, Dunkirk was a family tragedy. On 1 June he had haunted Waterloo and Victoria railway stations seeking news from the evacuated soldiers of his wife Eileen's beloved brother Laurence (Eric) O'Shaughnessy. 'Quite impossible, of course,' he wrote. 'The men who have been repatriated have orders not to speak to civilians and are in any case removed from the railway stations as promptly as possible.' Orwell's search was in vain. Eric O'Shaughnessy, a distinguished chest and heart surgeon who had been Orwell's only doctor since his return from Spain, was staunchly anti-fascist and had joined the Royal Army Medical Corps at the outbreak of war. O'Shaughnessy had approved of Orwell's 'warrior cast of mind' and his decision to fight in the Spanish Civil War, and when the Second World War broke out he had himself been determined to play his part in 'stopping Hitler'.[8] Major O'Shaughnessy was killed in Dunkirk by shrapnel during a bombing raid. Eileen was devastated. Tosco Fyvel described her sitting in silence when she and Orwell visited him, while another friend recorded that 'her grip on life, which had never been firm, loosened considerably'.[9] A third testified that she became 'almost mute'.[10] Lydia Jackson summed up Eric O'Shaughnessy's importance to his sister: 'I remember her telling me that she was sure that if anything untoward ever happened to her and she sent an appeal to her brother, he would come at once. She said that she wasn't so sure her husband would do this, that his work came before anybody.'[11]

Two days before Orwell revealed his Hebridean dream in his diary, Churchill had broadcast to the nation: 'The Battle of Britain is about to begin ... The whole fury and might of the enemy must very soon be turned on us.' In prose worthy of gracing the dust jacket of *Nineteen Eighty-Four*, Churchill warned that the world might 'sink into the abyss of a new dark age made more sinister, and perhaps more protracted, by the lights of perverted science'. Ten days previously, Orwell had warned the readers of a literary magazine, 'The future, at any rate the immediate future is not with the "sensible" men. The future is with the fanatics.'[12]

Living under the shadow of Nazi invasion, having lost a loved brother-in-law and comforting a heartbroken wife, it is no wonder that Orwell dreamed of leaving shabby, blacked-out, and soon to be bombed-out, London with its shortages of food and fuel, for the calm of 'my island in the Hebrides'. But a man who had single-mindedly headed towards the sound of gunfire to defend democracy and the Spanish Republic from fascism was not a man to flee London as Nazi bombs rained down on the city. His friend, the writer Julian Symons, recalled: 'I remember during the war, near the end of the war, going out to one of our weekly lunches, when he said to me how much he hated London, and how much he'd like to get out of it, "but of course" he said, "you can't get out, you can't leave when people are being bombed to bits all around you." He didn't say this in then least heroically. I would happily got out if I could have done.'[13] Poet Paul Potts, another friend of the countryside-loving Orwell, maintained that 'The only time he liked London was during the blitz.'[14]

'As I write,' began an essay by Orwell, 'civilized human beings are flying overhead, trying to kill me.' The Blitz had begun but Orwell wasn't staying on in London to witness the horrors in the spirit of writers seeking material. He patriotically wanted to 'do his bit'. He joined the Regent's Park unit of Local Defence Volunteers, soon re-named the Home Guard, bringing to the fledgling 'Dad's Army' his training with Eton's Officer Training Corps and the Indian police and actual battle experience in Spain, and earning himself the three stripes of a platoon sergeant. Orwell always had 'something in the nature of a military bearing', observed Rayner Heppenstall.

Orwell was 'almost certain' that England would be invaded. Recalling that he had a 'front seat view' of street fighting in Barcelona, he argued that 'a few hundred men with machine guns can paralyse the life of a large city' and recommended that the government arm civilians with hand grenades and shotguns from sporting shops.[15] In short, he demanded the government 'ARM THE PEOPLE' and personally instructed Home Guard units on street-fighting tactics.

Orwell had put aside the writing of novels, believing that, as well as being a paper shortage, 'Literature as we know it is coming to an end. Things look rather black at the moment.'[16] But early in 1941 he published *The Lion and the Unicorn*, a long essay in which he argued that class-ridden Britain needed a socialist revolution before it could beat Nazi Germany.

In late June 1941, Orwell watched British communists perform remarkable feats of ideological contortion to move from condemning a 'capitalist war' to supporting it. The cause of these acrobatics was Hitler tearing up his non-aggression pact with Stalin and the Nazi invasion of the Soviet Union. Stalin was now 'on our side' and had become widely popular among Britain's non-communist population. Orwell fumed: 'One could not have a better example of the moral and emotional shallowness of our time, than the fact that we are now all more or less pro-Stalin. This disgusting murderer is temporarily on our side, and so the purges, etc., are suddenly forgotten.'[17] If the anger that had burned within Orwell since he had witnessed – and only narrowly escaped – the Stalinist purge in Barcelona had ever needed rekindling, public admiration for the Soviet dictator now fanned the flame of his fury. This anger eventually spawned a novel that was destined to become a classic of English literature. What became *Animal Farm* had first entered Orwell's head in 1937, where it evolved until he finally sat down to commit it to paper around the end of 1943. After a five-year break from writing fiction, it would be unlike anything he had written before.

During the summer of that year Orwell took on a job as a Talks Assistant at the BBC, producing programmes for the Indian service in the belief that pontifications by T.S. Eliot and E.M. Forster would keep that vast nation on-side against the Japanese during Britain's time of peril. The fact that Orwell's *Burmese Days* had been thought subversive and initially banned in India seems to have been forgiven or forgotten. For the second time in his life Orwell was in the service of empire. The free spirit had entered a world of hierarchy, bureaucracy and censorship. The pay was good – £640 a year – but for a man who believed in Indian independence and that British rule there was 'just as bad as German Fascism', it was a distasteful venture into the world of propaganda. 'Two wasted years', he called it and described the atmosphere as 'something halfway between a girl's school and a lunatic asylum'. But it was an experience that he would draw on in *Nineteen Eighty-Four* as he created the sinister Ministry of Truth. 'One rapidly becomes propaganda-minded and develops a cunning one did not previously have', he reflected in his diary. It is said that Orwell attended compulsory editorial meetings in Room 101 of the BBC's Portland Place building. On Jura, Orwell later wrote: '"You asked me once," said O'Brien, "what was in Room 101. I told you that you knew the answer already. Everyone knows it. The thing that is in Room 101 is the worst thing in the world."'

Former BBC employees recognised the austere wartime canteen they and Orwell ate in in his description of the Ministry of Truth canteen in *Nineteen Eighty-Four*: 'A low ceilinged crowded room, its wall grimy from the contact of innumerable bodies; battered metal tables and chairs, placed so close together that you sat with your elbows touching; bent spoons, dented trays, coarse white mugs ...' Ironically, the BBC commemorates Orwell's 'wasted years' with a statue of its ungrateful employee outside Broadcasting House in London.

Wartime London could be a convivial place, despite the bombing and hardship, and Orwell was introduced to David Astor, a young Royal Marines officer, by his old friend Cyril Connolly.

Astor, who had been wounded in France and awarded the Croix de Guerre, was an Eton-educated, left-leaning liberal whose father happened to be a wealthy member of the House of Lords and owner of *The Observer*. David took an active role in the newspaper even during the war and went on to edit it for twenty-seven years. His mother was Nancy Astor, the first woman to sit in the House of Commons when she won her husband's Plymouth seat after he succeeded to the peerage on the death of his father.[18] David Astor had asked Connolly to recommend to him a writer 'good on politics' and when Connolly introduced him to Orwell over lunch at the Langham Hotel in Portland Place the pair immediately hit it off. 'I felt I'd known him all my life,' Astor recalled. Astor, brought up in the luxury of the family estate at Cliveden in Buckinghamshire, sometimes stayed at George and Eileen's spartan flat during the blackout where they would talk late into the night before Astor crashed out on a camp bed. Nine years Orwell's junior and from an uber-rich background, Astor nevertheless found what he called a 'kindred spirit'. The friendship had important consequences for Orwell. *The Observer* offered the writer a nationwide platform and Orwell's first article for it appeared in 1942. Furthermore, the Astor family had an estate on the Hebridean island of Jura, where David had spent many youthful holidays. Orwell's road to Jura began in the restaurant of the Langham Hotel where he met the man who would become a patron and a lifelong friend.

In March 1943 Orwell's mother Ida, who suffered from breathing difficulties, died in a Hampstead hospital with George at her side. Her death certificate cites heart failure, but also lists bronchitis and emphysema as secondary causes. Orwell had always been much closer to his mother than to his father, but it seems likely that he also inherited a respiratory weakness from her. He certainly had a bad attack of bronchitis that year and left the Home

Guard for medical reasons as well as resigning from the BBC on the grounds that very few Indians listened to the broadcasts he prepared. He joined the socialist weekly magazine *Tribune* as literary editor, giving up the five-and-a-half-day week at the BBC for a three-day week at *Tribune*. The pay was much less but it gave him the space to write a novel that would be unlike anything he had ever written before, *Animal Farm*.

*

In Barcelona, Orwell had witnessed a possible future: 'Above all, there was a belief in the revolution and the future, a feeling of having suddenly emerged into an era of equality and freedom. Human beings were trying to behave as human beings and not as cogs in the capitalist machine.' Since leaving Spain he had pondered on the betrayal of that revolution, and he had nursed the idea of a novel on that theme that drew on Orwell's love of Swift's *Gulliver's Travels*, a favourite since he was eight years old. 'It is a book,' he wrote, 'which it seems impossible for me to grow tired of.'[19] In the first part of *Gulliver*, Swift had satirised the court of Queen Anne, and it was with the weapon of satire that Orwell would savage the Russia of Joseph Stalin.

Subtitled 'A Fairy Story', *Animal Farm* is an allegory in which the descent of the Russian Revolution into Stalinist despotism is lampooned in a tale in which farm animals revolt against their owner, only to have the pigs inexorably replace the farmer as the masters. Farmer Jones represents Tsar Nicholas II, while pigs Old Major, Napoleon and Snowball are cast in the roles of Marx (perhaps with a touch of Lenin), Stalin and Trotsky. Poor Boxer the horse ('I will work harder ... Comrade Napoleon is always right'), who is worked to near death and then sent off to the knacker's yard by the pigs, represents the Russian masses. It was witnessing a small boy leading a powerful carthorse that had got Orwell wondering: 'What if it was to rebel?' It is a thought that doubtless occurred to him while serving in the minuscule Burma police force that controlled the Burma masses.

What is most remarkable about the book is that Orwell wrote it during the war, when the Soviet Union was Britain's ally and Stalin a popular figure among the British left. Scottish poet and songwriter Hamish Henderson's 'Ballad of the Taxi Driver's Cap' celebrated the troops' fondness for their ally 'Uncle Joe' Stalin.

> O Hitler's a non-smoker and Churchill smokes cigars,
> And they're both as keen as mustard on imperialistic wars.
> But your Uncle Joe's a worker and a very decent chap,
> Because he smokes a pipe and wears a taxi driver's cap.

On 28 July 1944 George and Eileen's top-floor flat was seriously damaged by a V-1 'doodlebug' flying bomb. Fortunately, the couple were away but the roof collapsed, destroying many of Orwell books and leaving his manuscript of *Animal Farm* in a 'slightly crumpled condition'. There is no doubt that such incidents and the general grimness of London life during the war shaped the new novel that was beginning to take shape in his mind, and he would inflict this misery on Winston Smith in *Nineteen Eighty-Four*:

This, he thought with a sort of vague distaste – this was London, chief city of Airstrip One, itself the third most populous of the provinces of Oceania. He tried to squeeze out some childhood memory that should tell him whether London had always been quite like this. Were there always these vistas of rotting nineteenth-century houses, their sides shored up with baulks of timber, their windows patched with cardboard and their roofs with corrugated iron, their crazy garden walls sagging in all directions? And the bombed sites where the plaster dust swirled in the air and the willow-herb straggled over the heaps of rubble; and the places where the bombs had cleared a larger patch and there had sprung up sordid colonies of wooden dwellings like chicken-houses?

After a year of work, Orwell completed *Animal Farm* in February 1944 and began to seek a publisher for it. But *Animal Farm* had not only been in danger from Nazi Germany's 'doodle-bugs'. Stalin had many useful idiots in British publishing whose fears of straying from the party line almost caused the novel to be delivered stillborn. As Allied forces gathered in Britain to prepare for the D-Day landings, the Soviet Army was bleeding Germany dry on the Eastern Front. 'Uncle Joe' Stalin was a cherished ally and leftish publishers shied clear of angering him or the millions who admired him. Victor Gollancz, the man behind the Left Book Club, who had rejected *Homage to Catalonia* unread with the words 'I ought never to publish anything which could harm the fight against fascism', now rejected *Animal Farm*.[20] Gollancz now told Orwell: 'I could not possibly publish … a general attack of this nature.' Orwell lamented: 'The argument that to tell the truth would be "inopportune" or would "play into the hands of" somebody or other is felt to be inanswerable, and very few people are bothered by the prospect that the lies which they condone will get out of the newspapers and into the history books.'[21]

More rejections followed – from Nicholson & Watson, Jonathan Cape, William Collins, and T.S. Eliot at Faber & Faber (who had previously rejected *Down and Out in Paris and London*). The Diall Press in New York rejected it because it 'was impossible to sell animal stories in the USA'. Eventually the left-wing, but anti-communist, Secker & Warburg accepted *Animal Farm*, although Fredric Warburg, who thought it a masterpiece, faced a lot of resistance including that of his wife Pamela who threatened to leave him if he published it.[22] But although spurned during the war and, as Orwell feared, 'bound to be a failure', his new novel would catch the mood of the Cold War and has been hailed as a classic ever since.

Animal Farm, Orwell wrote, 'was the first book in which I tried, with full consciousness of what I was doing to fuse political purpose and artistic purpose into one whole'. For Orwell, literature could no longer be simply entertainment; its role was to look unflinchingly into humankind's potential for the exploitation of and cruelty to its own kind. Those familiar with Orwell's previous work were amazed by its style and light touch. To Malcolm Muggeridge, the novel was a masterpiece: 'That book, like *Gulliver's Travels*, will always be of interest to people. It's beautifully worked out. Actually, I think George was better writing about animals than human beings, because the people in his novels aren't really convincing – but the animals were perfectly convincing! I think he had a sympathy with them.'[23] To Julian Symons, it was typical of Orwell that he wrote 'this anti-Stalinist satire in 1942, at the time when the Soviet Union probably reached its highest point of popularity in this country'.[24]

In *Animal Farm* Orwell achieved his ambition to make political writing into an art – and he had written a book that matched that of his beloved Jonathan Swift's. He wrote of Swift's master work: 'The durability of *Gulliver's Travels* goes to show that if the force of belief is behind it, a world-view which only just passes the test of sanity is sufficient to produce a great work of art.'[25] His own *Animal Farm* is such a book.

Swiftian satire? Absolutely. Coruscating take-down of the Russian Revolution? Without doubt. But *Animal Farm*, inspired by a small boy leading a powerful carthorse, could only have been written by a countryman. Orwell hated London, and he dreamed of getting out of it. He dreamed of the Hebrides.

CHAPTER 6

My Island in the Hebrides

'We in dreams behold the Hebrides.'

—*Canadian Boat-Song*, Anonymous

The year Nazism was finally overthrown should have been a high point in the war-weary writer's life. He had a loving and supportive wife, a successful book behind him and, at last, a child whom he and Eileen had adopted. Orwell had long wished to be a father and Tosco Fyvel recalled him chuckling with joy as he played with Fyvel's baby daughter. Rayner Heppenstall thought Orwell was 'miserable' about being childless, but Orwell confided to him that he believed himself to be sterile although there is no evidence of this. 'I have never undergone the examination because it is so disgusting,' he confided to a friend.[1] Eileen had gynaecological problems, suffering from ovation cysts and occasional unexplained bleeding, and may have been infertile. In her biography of Eileen, Sylvia Topp speculates that she suffered from endometriosis, a little understood condition in the 1940s. But wherever the problem lay Orwell took the responsibility for the lack of a child upon himself.

Orwell had set his heart on adopting a baby boy, and the fleeting nature of much wartime romance had ensured that unplanned infants were plentiful. It seems that Eileen was initially less keen on the idea, possibly because she was secretly concerned about her own health, her husband's health and coping with the demands of another needy male in her already stressful life. Orwell's desire for 'my island in the Hebrides' may also have worried her when she dwelt on the practicalities of caring for an infant and a husband with ramshackle health in a remote place, far from hospitals and the kind of care her late brother could have provided. Nevertheless, when Orwell's doctor sister-in-law – Gwen O'Shaughnessy, the widow of Eileen's brother – made the arrangement for George and Eileen to adopt a newborn baby boy, both parents adored him from the outset. In an act of powerful symbolism, Orwell burned the names of the child's natural parents from his birth certificate with a cigarette end.[2] The baby was now theirs, and theirs alone. They named him Richard Horatio Blair. Eileen's friend Lydia Jackson witnessed the new parents in action: '[Eileen] had bathed the baby and was giving him his bottle. George was kneeling before her, watching, entranced, rather in the manner of an adoring shepherd in a Nativity painting.'[3]

Orwell had not only become a parent but was a father who was soon able to provide adequately for his family. The little 'squib' (as he called *Animal Farm*) had flown off booksellers' shelves like some 'off-the-ration-book' delicacy, even though Orwell had to spend a day rushing around London bookshops removing it from the children's section shelves. He needn't have worried. *Animal Farm* was an instant best-seller and far outstripped his previous novels in both literary quality and popularity and made Orwell more financially secure than ever before. The book was an even greater success in America where the first print run was 50,000.

While he was writing it, Eileen had been working at the Ministry of Food and her colleague Lettice Cooper recalled her at coffee breaks quoting the latest passages of the book that Orwell had read aloud to her the previous night in bed.[4] Cooper thought Eileen was a good critic of her husband's writing, and Tosco Fyvel was convinced that Eileen's influence on her husband's work had given *Animal Farm* 'the light touch of her bright, humorous intelligence',[5] Eileen was certainly excited by the work, and Margaret Branch also recalled Eileen saying how she would amuse her fellow workers at the Ministry of Food by telling them what George had just written.[6]

With a best-selling novel behind him and royalties pouring in, Orwell was now in a position to make his Hebridean dream come true. The choice of the island of Jura was serendipitous – recommended to him by his friend David Astor as a place to take a break. Astor recalled: 'I never imagined he'd stay there. I only suggested that he go there for a short holiday because he obviously needed a holiday.' The well-intentioned Astor knew Jura well. As well as owning *The Observer*, David's fabulously rich father also owned the Tarbert estate on the island where David, his sister and three brothers had spent many happy childhood summers.

Jura was less popular with the children's mother, the formidable Lady Astor, and her lady's maid Rosina (Rose) Harrison who wrote less than favourable accounts of the holidays that the Astors either loved or endured at Tarbert Lodge. More like a farmhouse than a lordly manor, Rose thought the lodge spartan, 'not a place to be lived in, more one to come back to after a day's sport'. In a photograph in the book Rose wrote about her time with the Astors, she is seen sitting on a rocky shore with one of the estate's ghillies. The caption reads: 'This was a splendid sporting place for the gentlemen, but very boring for Lady Astor and me.'[7] Rose thought Tarbert Lodge 'in the middle of nowhere' and missed the excitement of London and the companionship of the Cliveden family estate. On one occasion Lady Astor gave vent to her feelings about the place by whacking golf balls at the house, two of which broke windows. 'I think I know how she felt,' wrote Rose.

Rose thought Jura was ideal for the Astor children with swimming, climbing, walking, deerstalking and fishing. Fishing, to Rose, was 'a nasty, monotonous, slimy business conducted in the cold and the wet, and can be downright dangerous'. And while she liked fresh mackerel, she became scunnered with them for breakfast every morning. While Lord Astor made a point of dining daily on the venison and seafood of Jura, he was very particular about the milk his children drank there, and when the family travelled to Jura they were always accompanied by a cow and cowman from the Home Farm at Cliveden. The cow travelled in a wagon at the end of the train, and Rose remembered it being milked on a station platform.[8] With a young infant, Orwell too would become fixated on milk while living on Jura, walking a mile for it and seeking to buy a TB-tested cow.

Biographers have sometimes put Orwell's first visit to Jura in September 1945, but we now know that he went there a full year earlier. The first clue to this is an inconsequential business-like letter to T.S. Eliot, written on 5 September 1944, in which Orwell mentioned in passing that 'I am going away for the second half of September …' But where? Orwell's diaries and letters are mute about this trip, but a letter Eileen wrote to him on 21 March 1945 makes it clear that arrangements to rent and repair Barnhill farmhouse (at a cost of £200) were well advanced, nearly six months before his supposed first arrival there. Could such arrangements been made without Orwell having seen Barnhill and met its owners in person? It seems unlikely.

There is also written evidence for Orwell's 1944 visit to Jura in the autobiography of the great English film director Michael Powell. That year Powell and his creative partner Emeric Pressburger were marking time until the funds were available to buy the Technicolor film stock with which they would shoot their masterpiece, *A Matter of Life and Death*. With time on their hands, they decided to make a film on an idea of Pressburger's about a girl's obsession to get to a remote Island and the difficulties she would encounter. The filmmakers began to scout locations for what would become the classic romance *I Know Where I'm Going!*, starring Wendy Hiller and Roger Livesey.[9] Prior to the cameras rolling in the autumn of 1944, Powel had turned up at Crinan on the Argyll mainland and, with a five-pound note, persuaded a local man with a boat to take him across to Jura. Powell was an islomaniac whose passion for islands had taken him to live and film on Fula, the most remote of the Shetland Isles, to make his first on-location feature film *The Edge of the World*, which he was inspired to make after reading about the evacuation of St Kilda. Powell's plan for Jura was to find somewhere to sleep that night and the following morning to walk to the south of the island and then cross the narrow straight to Islay, where he would meet his wife Frankie at the Port Askaig Hotel. Being put ashore on Jura, he encountered a reticent couple who, on finding that he was a film director whose movies they loved, warmed to him and invited him to stay the night. As the evening progressed and drams were downed, it became clear that the couple's relationship was secretive and most likely not quite respectable, but Powell – no stranger to extra-marital love affairs himself – declared that war banished conventions and that 'he is a fool who hesitates in love or war'.

Powell's autobiography is admirably coy about identifying these lovebirds but infuriatingly vague about where their house was or exactly when the evening of whisky-inspired confidences took place. The following morning, Powell and his host took a path to climb the Paps of Jura, with Powell observing as they passed 'the stalker's cottage … a modest house with a slate roof' from which smoke was rising from the chimney. Powell's ears pricked up at his companion's mention of a writer called Blair living there. 'Not Eric Blair?' he asked, later describing his question as a shot in the dark. And, of course, it was. Powell told his host that one day the cottage would become a place of literary pilgrimage and, after exploring the Paps and crossing to Port Askaig, Powell told his wife who was waiting for him in the hotel that he had nearly met George Orwell.

In November, as soon as location filming was complete, Powell went directly to Denham Studios in Buckinghamshire to shoot the film's interior scenes and the tank shots in which the leading actors were tossed around in a small boat while being assailed by wind machines and stagehands throwing buckets of water at them against back-projected images of the Corryvreckan whirl-pool – for the scene in which the soon-to-be lovers are almost drowned in the very same maelstrom that would almost kill George Orwell.[10]

And so the 'what ifs?' What if the two men had met? What if the persuasive Michael Powell had got Orwell to talk about the book he was writing? What if the two men had signed a movie deal? Orwell had once been a film critic and would certainly have known Powell's reputation, and Powell admired Orwell and was a direc-tor who relished a challenge. He was at the height of his creative powers and his next film, *A Matter of Life and Death*, proved that Orwell's *Nineteen Eighty-Four* was certainly within the capability of Powell and Emeric Pressburger. But Michael Powell passed by the 'stalker's cottage' that day on Jura, and the great director and the great novelist never met.[11] Orwell would have been happy for his book to have been made into a film. He thought it was 'filmable' and told his agent Leonard Moore that while he couldn't collab-orate on such a project, he would have to see the script before it was made.[12] A forgettable film of the book was made in 1954 and a groundbreaking BBC drama followed in 1956, but it wasn't until the year 1984 itself that a cinema version worthy of Powell and Pressburger was finally directed by Michael Radford.

But what of the 'stalkers cottage'? Knowing no one on Jura, Orwell had turned to David Astor for help finding accommoda-tion. Astor contacted Janet MacKinnon, who helped out at his family's Tarbert estate house, asking her if his friend could stay with her family. Janet's family had been on the island for genera-tions and their home had been a simple cottage at Corrynahera, near Lagg, now a ruin. Fiona Fletcher, first-born of Margaret and Robin Fletcher, who would eventually become Orwell's Barnhill landlords, remembers it well: 'It was a "but 'n' ben" with a wee hoosie [outside toilet] out the back over a stream. I thought it was fascinating.' Fiona believes, however, that the house Orwell would have stayed at is the one that Janet later moved to near the shore at Tarbert when she married postman Calum MacKinnon. Could this have been where Orwell stayed in September 1944, and perhaps when he visited again a year later? Both Lagg and Tarbert are not far from the Corran River bridge from where people traditionally climb the Paps of Jura, and Michael Powell would certainly have passed through them.

Janet and Calum were reluctant landlords. 'At first they said no, they couldn't do it,' said Astor, but he persisted and finally Janet agreed. Astor recalled:

> George went off. I heard nothing from him. Then I discovered he had found an empty farmhouse while he was there and had applied to the landowner asking if he could rent it. I was horrified when I heard this. It was an extremely uncomfortable place to live. There was only one doctor on the island, no telephone and no proper road. For a person in delicate health it was a crazy place to go, but he was very independent; I would never have dared to advise him against settling there. But then I didn't know how ill he was. If I had, I think I would have said, 'This is crazy.'[13]

The empty farmhouse Orwell had discovered at the far north end of Jura was Barnhill. It wasn't on the Astor estate but owned by the Fletchers of Ardlussa, the near neighbours of the Astors – in as much that Highland estate owners have near neighbours. Ardlussa's 'chatelaine' was Margaret Fletcher, who had married Robin Fletcher in 1938. Margaret's father, Walter Hargreaves Brown, had bought the Ardlussa estate from the Astors, and then merged it with the neighbouring Barnhill estate under the Ardlussa title. Margaret had inherited the combined property when her brother Sandy, a lieutenant in the Scots Guards, was killed in action in October 1944. Margaret revealed that Orwell had written to her brother Sandy earlier that year 'to find out if there was a suitable house to rent'. When Margaret returned to Jura the following year to live with her husband Robin and young children, Orwell renewed the correspondence. Barnhill had lain empty throughout the war years and the Fletchers were happy for it to be lived in again rather than go to wrack and ruin, and they offered it to Orwell at a very low rent.

*

Jura is the fourth largest island of the Inner Hebrides, after Skye, Mull and Islay. A little over twenty-seven miles long, its 140 square miles are comprised mainly of a huge wedge of metamorphic Jura Quartzite that reaches its maximum height at the famous Paps of Jura – distinctly breast-shaped mountains but, confusingly, three in number. The unforgiving rock leaves little room for arable land, and farming is confined to some glacial till on a narrow strip down the east coast. The mountains are left to the numerous red deer and the stalkers who shoot them. The very name Jura may be Viking in origin and derived from the Old Norse for 'Deer Island'. The island benefits from being washed by the warming Gulf Stream and lying snow is rare and frost short lived, but the prevailing westerly winds are rain-laden and frequently drench Jura's mountains. Orwell himself wrote: 'The climate, although wet, is not quite so cold as England, and it is much easier to get fuel …'[14]

After years in London Orwell was excited by the prospect of the combined writing and outdoor life he could enjoy on Jura and the freedom it would give their son. In September 1945, Orwell headed – for the second time – to Jura and spent twelve days there. He proposed spending the summer of 1946 at Barnhill, and Eileen wrote to Margaret Fletcher about the practicalities of living there: what was already in the house, what should she bring, how and where were the daily necessities purchased? Margaret Fletcher told biographer Bernard Crick: 'I liked her instantly from the letter.' In 1980 Margaret Fletcher, by then widowed and now Margaret Nelson, told Crick that she got the impression that Eileen was less enthusiastic about the move than her husband, and suggested that Eileen should visit Jura before making a decision to move there. However, with its five bedrooms, bathroom, hot and cold running water, large sitting room and kitchen, Barnhill was luxurious compared to the tin-roofed cottage in Wallington, leading Eileen to comment favourably on the place: it was 'just what we wanted to live in twelve months of the year'.[15] Orwell replied to Margaret Fletcher saying that Eileen was having an operation, but that they would visit Jura for ten days once she had recovered.[16]

In February 1945 Orwell had resolved to see something of the war in Europe for himself and witness the collapse of a dictatorship. He planned a two-month stint in Europe as a war correspondent for *The Observer* while Eileen and baby Richard stayed near Newcastle and Eileen's sister-in-law Gwen O'Shaughnessy, from where Eileen was able to write to George that Richard had started to crawl. Like Orwell, Eileen had always refused to submit to any illness until it became debilitating, and in Newcastle she suffered anaemia, regular bleeding and exhaustion. As baby Richard healthily put on weight, his mother declined. True to form, she stoically kept 'mum' about it to Orwell.

Orwell never got close to the fighting but filed stories revealing the conditions of civilians in Germany, Austria and France. In Paris he met Ernest Hemingway, who had been in Spain during the civil war as an imbedded journalist with the Soviet-supported International Brigades. Hemingway later wrote that Orwell confided in him that he feared assassination for his attacks on

Stalinism by the same forces that had hunted him in Barcelona and had borrowed a Colt .32 from him for his self-protection. Orwell – whose understanding of totalitarianism had hitherto been shaped by Stalinism rather than Hitlerism – hoped to be in Berlin for the Allied endgame and witness the final capitulation of the Nazis, but a severe attack of bronchitis detained him in Cologne where at one stage he believed he would die.[17] The lines he had not long written about the death of the loyal horse Boxer in *Animal Farm* had come close to prediction: 'A thin stream of blood had trickled out of his mouth … "It's my lung," said Boxer in a weak voice.' As Orwell recovered, he received the terrible news in a telegram from *The Observer* that Eileen had died.

Eileen had been found to have tumours in her uterus and had agreed to a hysterectomy, a serious but routine operation. As she lay in bed waiting to be wheeled into the operating theatre, she began writing a letter to George while her anaesthetic injection took effect. She planned to complete the letter when she awoke after the operation. She never did. At just thirty-nine, Eileen had a heart attack and died while under anaesthetic on 29 March 1945. Like Orwell, she had been careless of her health, smoking heavily and skimping on health care in those pre-NHS days. While she nursed her husband through illness and haemorrhage, he had been seemingly oblivious to her health. Eileen's friend Lydia Jackson recalled: 'I was always sorry that Eileen married George. She deserved someone who would support her. I think his work was all to him, human relationships just a background. She really needed and deserved devotion, I think.'[18] But perhaps Orwell just was emotionally stymied by an upper-middle-class English reticence and found it difficult to express his feelings. Paul Potts recalled that Orwell 'told me the last time he saw her he wanted to tell her that he loved her much more now since they'd had Richard, and he didn't tell her, and he regretted it immensely'.[19]

Orwell – now a grieving widower and the single parent of a ten-month-old baby – begged a lift on a military aircraft and flew home. Not given to outbursts of emotion, he seemed stoic, but friends detected the pain beneath the stiff-upper-Etonian-lip. Paul Potts testified: 'Theirs was a real marriage ... not perfect. But nothing except her death, that came so suddenly and too early, would have broken it up.' Orwell himself wrote to a friend: I was sometimes unfaithful to Eileen, and I also treated her badly, and I think she treated me badly, too, at times, but it was a real marriage, in the sense that we had been through awful struggles together and she understood all about my work, etc.'[20] When offered condolences, Orwell would mutter brief thanks and change the subject, but his close friend Tosco Fyvel believed that he had been left desolate and grieved deeply. 'Eileen's death,' wrote Fyvel, 'was a blow to him from which he never recovered.'[21] John Morris, a former colleague at the BBC, thought that Orwell was 'a man of deep feelings, but he had an almost Oriental capacity for hiding his emotions ... I made what was undoubtedly a clumsy attempt to express my sympathy. "Yes," he said in reply, "it is most inconvenient. I don't know how I shall be able to look after the child."'[22]

Friends believed that he would have to give up Richard for re-adoption, but Orwell was proving to be a loving and competent father who had bonded with the infant and could change and bathe his baby and carry him easily on his hip, in an era when such skills were seldom found in men. He wrote to a friend: 'There really isn't anything left in my life except my work and seeing that Richard gets a good start.'[23] Anthony Powell recalled: 'Now that the child was part of the household, he was not going to relinquish him, no matter what the difficulties. In fact, one side of Orwell – the romantic side that played such a part – rather enjoyed the picture of himself coping unaided with a baby. Let this point be made clear: Orwell did cope with the baby. It may have been romanticism, but, if so, it was romanticism that found practical expression. This was characteristic of him in all he did. His idiosyncrasies were based in guts.'[24] Given that Orwell only really got to know his own father on his return from Burma and had no experience of a close father-son bond, his devotion to Richard and ability to care for him is a remarkable testimony to Orwell's deep humanity.

Looking after Richard, or Ricky as he was often called, gave Orwell a purpose in life, other than writing, that brought him joy. A few years later, when his friend Julian Symons announced that he was about to become a father, Orwell told him that babies were 'awful fun in spite of the nuisance'.[25] But Orwell was desperately lonely, vulnerable and concerned that his child was motherless. His strategy was to find a wife, and his tactic was to propose to women he hardly knew. 'What I am really asking you,' he wrote to one, 'is whither you would like to be the widow of a literary man.' He went on to offer the probability of royalties and promised that – as he thought himself sterile – he wouldn't be jealous if she had another man's child while married to him. 'I want peace and quiet and someone to be fond of me ...' he wrote pathetically.[26] Orwell asked several young women to marry him in similarly hasty style, but no avail. One was Sonia Brownell. Sonia was the much-desired literary assistant to Cyril Connolly, an old schoolfriend of Orwell's and the editor of the influential magazine *Horizon*. Sonia may have consented to sleep with Orwell but refused marriage at this time.

Wifeless, Orwell acquired a live-in housekeeper who joined him and Ricky in the writer's bleak flat in Islington's Canonbury Square, where he and Eileen had moved after being bombed out by the 'doodlebug' flying bomb. Susan Watson was twenty-seven, separated from her husband and had a seven-year-old daughter who was at boarding school. She came from a highly educated family, had met Jacob Epstein and Ludwig Wittgenstein, was used to intellectual types and was an astute observer of her new employer. She told the 1983 BBC *Arena* documentary series about Orwell: 'He was an interesting man to be with. He was very rigid about the routine of his domestic life. He expected things to be done exactly to time. But he was a nice man to work for, but not easy.' Questioned if he was a stickler for order, she replied: 'Ah, yes. Order and time, and he worked tremendously hard. I mean he started off working about half past eight in the morning and then he'd stop for lunch. Usually, he went out for lunch. He'd come back about two and work till about six.'[27]

A habitual workaholic, Orwell's loneliness after Eileen's death meant he buried himself deeper into work. Since *Animal Farm* had made him famous, newspapers and magazines craved articles from him, all sorts of societies sought him as a speaker and the BBC wanted him to write scripts. But *Animal Farm* had made him financially secure for the first time since resigning from the Burma police and had given him access to a precious commodity: time. With a new novel forming in his mind, he, at last, had the opportunity to get away from the tyranny of earning a living and write it.

Orwell's dream of his Hebridean island had not died with Eileen. As 1946 dawned, he made definite plans to move to Jura and clear his desk and mind to make way for the novel he planned to call *The Last Man in Europe*. 'I am going to stop doing the *Evening Standard* stuff and most other journalism in May and take six months off to write another novel. If the Jura place can be put in order this year I shall go there … I am constantly smothered under journalism – at present I am doing 4 articles every week … I feel desperately tired and jaded.'[28]

Orwell's friend Tosco Fyvel recalled many years later that he was not surprised by Orwell's move to Jura: 'My wife and I felt very protective towards him because I somehow felt after his wife

Eileen's death his life in London where he was busily saying "yes" to all journalism commissions and writing and writing, it somehow wasn't viable. I could see why he sort of walked out on this and went all the way to Jura.'[29]

Another priority was to get twenty-one-month-old Richard, now 'a big strong child … active and intelligent', out of London and in February Orwell was fretting that the Fletchers would not have Barnhill, unoccupied for six years, in a fit state for him to move in to. The Fletchers, however, were keen to have a tenant and got to work. Margaret Fletcher remembered: 'We rather enjoyed the challenge of trying to get it ready. We were very enthusiastic about getting the estate going, getting people back to work here.' By the end of March, the house was ready, and Orwell was arranging to send his furniture to Jura and planning a two-month break from writing once he and Richard got there. Writing to Stafford Cottman,[30] an old comrade with whom he served alongside in Spain and made his escape with as the communists purged the POUM members in Barcelona, Orwell made his plans clear:

> I have given up the cottage in Hertfordshire and taken another in the island of Jura in the Hebrides, and hope to go up there about May 10th if my furniture has arrived by that time. It's in an extremely un-getatable place, but it's a nice house and I think I can make it quite comfortable with a little trouble, and then I shall have a nice place to retire to occasionally at almost no rent. My little boy … is now nearly two and extremely active, which is one of the reasons why I am anxious to get out of London for the summer.[31]

On 3 May Orwell's older sister Marjorie died of kidney disease at just forty-eight. In a little over three years Orwell had lost his mother, wife and older sister. Days after her funeral, the writer set off for Barnhill, visiting Eileen's grave near Newcastle on the way and dropping by his Spanish Civil War comrade and commander Georges Kopp, who had taken on a tenant farm near Biggar in the Scottish Borders. In a strange twist of fate, Kopp had married Gwen O'Shaughnessy's half-sister Doreen, so Orwell had a double connection to the couple.[32]

On 22 May 1946, a day that he recalled was 'fine but not very warm', Orwell travelled by train to Glasgow and on to Gourock (which he spells 'Gouuroch' in his diary) to catch the 'steamer' (as even oil-fired boats were called on the west coast) to Dunoon and then on via Colintraive and Tighnabruaich to East Loch Tarbert on Loch Fyne. From there he travelled another further five miles by bus to West Loch Tarbert to board the MV *Locheil*, the long-serving ferry and mail boat operated by David MacBrayne Limited that served the island of Islay and Craighouse on the south of Jura. Orwell always advised his guests to travel third class on the vessel – there only were first and third class – because there was no difference in the food except that first class passengers enjoyed silver service. The food, he told former lover Sally McEwan, 'is filthy anyway'.

To this day Craighouse boasts Jura's only shop (now community owned) and in Orwell's time also enjoyed the luxuries of a rare telephone and an elderly GP. Fiona, the oldest of Margaret and Robin Fletcher's children, recalls him as 'Dear old Doctor Sandeman – not a modern doctor and very elderly. He would never have gone to Barnhill.'

Along twenty miles of winding, north-bound, single-track road lay Ardlussa, the home of Orwell's Fletcher landlords, and seven miles beyond that, at the end of a track impassable to most vehicles, Barnhill farmhouse. Orwell took the post-van to Ardlussa where Margaret Fletcher had offered to put him up on his first night. She recalled: 'He arrived at the front door looking very thin and gaunt and worn. I was immediately struck by the very sad face he had … He was tall and dark and very haggard looking and a very sick-looking man. He looked as if he had been through a great deal.'[33]

For better or for worse, Orwell's dream of living on his island in the Hebrides had finally come true.

Part Two

KEN CRAIG (CREATIVE COMMONS)

CHAPTER 7

Barnhill: Not an Impossible Journey

'I ought to have foreseen that he would contrive to find the most uninhabitable house in the British Isles.'

—Richard Rees

The morning after Orwell's arrival on Jura in May 1946, Margaret and Robin Fletcher drove the writer along the bumpy seven-mile track to lonely Barnhill. Despite the scarcity of building materials, and other properties on the estate also being in urgent need of repair, the couple had worked hard to make the house habitable, replacing slates, cleaning and painting rooms and even laying fires. Margaret recalled:

Eric started with very little furniture; he had only his basic needs – a camp bed, table, a chair or two and a few essential cooking utensils. We lent him some furniture and gradually more was obtained but even by the end of his time on Jura the house never looked comfortable and except for the warm fire his sister, Avril, had in the kitchen it was fairly bleak. It was certainly a spartan existence to begin with but it was the way he wanted to and gave the conditions under which he liked to work.[1]

Margaret showed the author around, but he was quick – even abrupt – in turning down her offer to help getting supplies, which were strictly rationed and difficult to obtain. 'Oh no, don't worry,' he told her, 'I'll manage myself. I'll manage myself.' She thought that he didn't mind being there alone as long as he 'had a roof over his head and a loaf of bread to chew on, but all the same it must have been difficult and lonely for him in that big old house'.

'His house was a well built one and it wasn't particularly uncomfortable,' attested David Astor, who had no idea when he recommended Jura to Orwell that the writer was tubercular and had spent time in a sanatorium. 'With hindsight, yes it was the wrong place to go. He should have been in a drier place, a more comfortable house and near to a doctor.' Richard Rees, who visited Orwell at Barnhill, remembered: 'When he told me he intended in future to spend the summers in a farmhouse on a Hebridean island I ought to have foreseen that he would contrive to find the most uninhabitable house in the British Isles. His letter inviting me to stay concluded with the ominous words: "It's quite an easy journey really, except that you have to walk the last eight miles."'[2]

Barnhill lies on the site of a fifteenth-century century settlement whose Gaelic name (Cnoc an t-Sabhail, 'Hill of the Barn') has been translated directly into English. Today, the exterior of Barnhill has changed little since Orwell's time, other than the removal of one of its three original chimney stacks by an Atlantic gale. It is a substantial mid nineteenth-century building, quite unusual on this island of traditional cottages. Downstairs lies a spacious living room and large kitchen/dining room with a pantry and laundry room. The kitchen was the centre of domestic life, leaving the chilly dining room to be used mostly as a summer guest bedroom. Upstairs are four smallish bedrooms, one (top left when you stand facing the front of the building) in which Orwell slept and did most of his writing. There were outbuildings and about sixteen acres of land that Orwell was free to farm if he wished. In front of the house lay a field where he established a garden, and beyond that the shore where he kept a dinghy for fishing – a dinghy that was almost his nemesis.

While Orwell was anxious to escape being 'smothered under journalism' he had no intention of cutting himself off from friends. The day after his arrival he wrote to Michael Meyer: 'I'm just settling in here – up to my eyes getting the house straight, but it's a lovely house … Come and stay sometime. It's not such an impossible journey (about 48 hours from London) and there's plenty of room in this house, though of course conditions are rough.'[3]

The 'rough conditions' include the fact that Jura was experiencing a drought and, while there was enough to drink, there wasn't enough water for baths. 'One doesn't get very dirty here,' Orwell promised, and given the smog and grime of London, he had a point. He had arrived alone, not with Richard and Susan Watson as he would have wished – as Susan had to stay in London for a minor operation and Orwell felt he couldn't cope on his own with settling in while looking after an active toddler – but planned to fetch them both from London later.

Furthermore, a motorbike was his only form of transport – 'hell on these roads', he noted. Orwell had become at least a competent motorcyclist in Burma but longed for a Jeep. Competent motorcyclist he may have been, but Margaret Fletcher decided he wasn't a competent mechanic as his machine constantly broke down and he would sit by the roadside for an hour or so fiddling with it before hiking to Ardlussa to find someone more mechanically minded. Fiona Fletcher, who was six or seven at the time, remembers urgent knocks at the door of Ardlussa and finding Orwell standing in the dark at the door, draped from head-to-toe in dripping black oilskins and with a sou'wester on his head. 'I was a little frightened of him,' she recalled.

His motorcycle would have broken down and he'd be looking for a lift to Barnhill. My father would take him, and mother wouldn't expect to see him again that night because they'd get stuck in a ditch in the dark and sit there all night just talking. Both were sociable and both were Etonians. Father had been in the Gordon Highlanders and captured in Singapore by the

Japanese and had been in Changi prison camp. I think they found each other interesting.[4]

Transport would always be a 'chief difficulty' for Orwell on Jura and even when he got a car the shortage of petrol and tyres remained a headache. In a very ruralist response to the problem, Orwell acquired Bob, a 'garron' or Highland pony, which willingly pulled a harrow but rebelled when hitched to a trap.

Ever the countryman, Orwell was quick to observe his surroundings. Jura, he noted in his dairy the day after his arrival, was enjoying a hot spell, with streams running dry and the fishermen blaming poor catches on the drought and the east wind. The trees, he observed, were gnarly and not very high, but fruit trees grew well in sheltered places. Azaleas, rhododendrons and fuchsias thrived, often growing wild like weeds, and primroses were still in full bloom.[5] There were bluebells in profusion, and thrift was in flower on the rocks of the shore with wild iris ready to bloom just above the high-tide mark. He shot a young rabbit for the pot, noting that the place was overrun by them. That day he wrote to his friend Michael Meyer about obtaining some percussion caps for his gun, admitting that he didn't have a firearms licence but saying: 'There's no policeman on the island!' He was making his own gunpowder – a skill he had learned as a boy addicted to causing explosions. 'A resourceful boy could make gunpowder for himself if he took the precaution of buying the ingredients from three different chemists,' he had written in an *Evening Standard* article about childhood pastimes.

The following day Orwell began the back-breaking job of stripping turf and turning over the stony, bone-dry soil to create a salad patch. He laid plans for his garden: 'This autumn shall put in bushes, rhubarb & fruit trees if possible, but it will need a very high and strong fence to keep the deer off them.' He had a go at cutting peat and although he must have relished the thought of free fuel, he noted that a family's annual supply cost a full month's hard work. His little parch of the Hebrides was to prove a tougher challenge than his garden in Wallington.

Orwell was used to roughing it. Life at Barnhill might be spartan, but it would be quiet and a clean and healthy place for Richard to grow up free and close to nature. 'I think he was determined that Richard should have a country life because he was worried Richard would get TB,' recalled Margaret Fletcher. 'I think Richard was uppermost in his concern.'

As a writer he had found a place where he could concentrate on the great work that was roiling away within his imagination. Orwell – always a man to dedicate himself fully – now committed himself to making his dream come true. In his 1946 essay *Why I Write* he stated that he had strong feelings about prose style, had a love for the surface of the earth and took pleasure in solid objects. On Jura the freedom to write uninterrupted, the joy of observing nature, fishing and gardening, and his desire to work with his hands could all be indulged, if he remained well enough.

With the aid of a six-inch-to-the-mile Ordnance Survey map, Orwell calculated the extent of Barnhill farm. 'Exclusive of the garden & the marshy field it appears to me to be just over 16 acres,' he concluded. With so much to do and to experience, Orwell postponed making a start on *Nineteen Eighty-Four*. The weeks that followed his arrival at the house were filled with settling in and establishing his garden, but he also took time to explore the west coast of Jura, on one occasion walking to Glengarrisdale and back, three hours each way, so was clearly enjoying reasonable health. At Glengarrisdale he found an old human skull which he believed to have been from a massacre of 'MacCleans' by the Campbells two centuries previously.

A week after Orwell arrived on Jura he was joined by his sister Avril. Alone since her mother died, Avril became the mistress – or at least the housekeeper – of Barnhill. She had been the joint-owner of *The Copper Kettle*, a successful teashop, and then had done war work in a sheet-metal factory, but from now on would devote herself to looking after her older brother and his son. In 1960 she told the BBC: 'He had previously asked me if I'd like to go up during the summer and give him a hand with helping in the house and helping with young Richard and so on. I was only too pleased. I'd just managed to escape from the essential works order – I'd been working in a factory all during the war and felt that really a spot of country air would just be the thing I wanted.'

In 1983 Margaret Fletcher told documentary makers: 'She came on holiday at first and then saw the situation there and decided to stay and look after Richard and housekeep for Eric. She was then mainstay of everything. Without her I don't think it would have been possible for them to have been up there. She was very practical. Great sense of humour about things.'[6]

Orwell spent £10 on a 12-foot dinghy and Avril bought two lobster creels. Orwell later noted that this investment 'easily repaid its original cost' in fish. On the 6 June Orwell boiled two lobsters and carefully noted down the price they would fetch at market (2s 11½d per pound). Orwell had loved fishing since he was a boy and on Jura fished regularly for the pot. Out in his dinghy half a dozen times in early July he never came home empty handed: 'Best catch (twice) 15 fish, 14 saythe & 1 pollock. Last night A[vril] caught a mackerel, but in picking it off the hook it got back into the water. Mackerel fishing proper starts in August. The fish always seem to bite about dusk, i.e., now about 11pm. There is a period of about 10 minutes when one is pulling them in for all one is worth, then they suddenly stop.'

Barnhill: Not an Impossible Journey

With no electricity, Barnhill was lit by candle and paraffin lamp. Candles were scarce and paraffin came in forty-gallon drums which needed manhandling to get to Barnhill. Orwell calculated that his stove and Aladdin lamps would require three gallons a week and that his forty-gallon drum would last him until the end of August. Coal was delivered to Jura by boat once a year, and Barnhill's ration came by tractor and trailer. From his diaries we can see that Orwell had arrived on Jura with a clear idea of the challenges of living in such a remote place and was able to summon the practicality and self-reliance required for such a life.

In early July Orwell went to London to collect Richard and Susan Watson and bring his son to his new home, carrying the not-yet-two-year-old down the last two miles of the rough track. For Susan, who walked with a limp due to childhood polio, the trek must have been hard. Orwell had found London 'unbearably hot' and noted in his diary that it been raining continually on Jura while he was away. Orwell's domestic diaries are just that – purely about the practicalities of living and nothing about his writing, family or friends. They are consequently both illuminating and frustrating. Fiona Fletcher was surprised at how dull the diaries were – for instance saying nothing about the drama when Richard gashed his head, which her mother helped patch up. 'They're all about gardening – and rabbits!' she told me.

As Avril enjoyed fishing, and Orwell intended to let Richard enjoy the outdoor life, we may assume that the trio were together on 12 July when the sea was alive with fish and the saithe were jumping around the boat. 'We could have caught 50 if we had wanted them,' he wrote, but added that they had not wanted to take more than they could eat and had packed up after catching twenty-four in twenty minutes. 'They are delicious eating,' he commented. 'Trying to find out exactly the method by which people here dry them for the winter.'

Shooting rabbits to eat – and to prevent them from eating his vegetables – was another outdoor occupation that Orwell enjoyed, and he experimented with ways to preserve their skins with which he planned to make a bed cover and slippers. Susan Watson recalled: 'George used to shoot rabbits on Jura and saltpeter the skins. He made himself a tobacco pouch of rabbit skin lined with an old piece of inner tube. Talk about old fashioned craftsmanship.'[7] Orwell noted in his diary: '1 small skin about large enough for a pouch. Made mustard spoon out of a deer's bone.'

Orwell's domestic diaries are full of sightings of birds and animals, and he noted that otters caught bigger lobsters than humans did – the ones too big to enter creels. 'Ditto salmon,' he noted. 'A 40 lb. salmon partly devoured by an otter is said to have been found here, no human being ever caught one of such size on this island.'

Living off the land was a preoccupation of Orwell's, and he was determined to try traditional Hebridean food. He noted in his diary: 'A[vril] procured some specimens of edible seaweed – dulse, not carragheen. She is drying it. Directions for preparing & cooking it vary somewhat, but it is said, when cooked in milk, to make a pudding rather like blancmange.' Susan Watson recalled that 'blancmange' with horror: 'He had this awful idea we would like carageen pudding. You go onto the seashore and pick up the seaweed; then you wash it and peg it on the line to dry; then you stew it. I thought it was disgusting stuff. I wouldn't eat it, but thought it was good and healthy.'

*

Today, around 200 people live on Jura – with fewer than a score of them Gaelic speakers, but none speaking the pure native dialect of Jura. But in 1946, when Orwell first rented the house at Barnhill, Jura was a Gaelic stronghold. The 1951 census shows that nearly fifty-nine per cent of the Diùraich (natives of Jura) had Gaelic – 155 of the 263 inhabitants. These would have been mostly small farmers, crofters, fishermen and tradesman – Scots far removed from the sons of toffs he met at St Cyprian's school and the racist planters he learned to despise in Burma. Orwell's exposure to these ordinary, down-to-earth, Gaelic-speaking Hebrideans changed him profoundly. His friend George Woodcock theorised that that the democratising influence of nonconformist sects and a much longer tradition of universal education in in Scotland had created a much less stratified society that enabled the shy and middle-class Orwell to get closer to the people of Jura than he could to the deeply class-conscious miners of Wigan.[8]

Decades of Scotophobia fell away as he got to know, and sometimes laboured with, people whose self-reliance, shy reticence and lack of a spurious sense of self-entitlement so echoed his own. To re-quote Christopher Hitchens, Orwell was 'A man arguing all the time with his own prejudices and his own fears, his own bigotries, his own shortcomings …' and he finally came to empathise with his new neighbours.[9] Orwell wrote with sympathy about the crofters' struggle to survive: 'Alistair and the D.s in a great state with the sheep. They are lambing in such a state of weakness that thy have no milk, sometimes actually refuse to take their lambs, & even now that the grass is coming on, some of them are too weak to graze. The D.s say the gulls & hoodies attack weak sheep, & yesterday took the eyes out of one of them.'[10]

Orwell met and was quickly befriended by his nearest neighbours, Donald Darroch and his sister Katie, who had a cottage two miles up the track at Kinauchdrachd, the most northerly house on Jura. Until he himself got a cow it was to the Darrochs' he went to most days to fetch milk. Donald's son, Donald Ewen Darroch, recalls his father's stories about Orwell:

Initially they thought he was quite a strange man. The first few times he came to get milk he just used to come and sit in the kitchen and wouldn't speak, so they thought he was quite droll. And it was only after that they learned that, because of his illness, he was actually quite breathless because of the long walk. There's quite a steep hill up straight up to Kinauchdrachd and that's why he came in and just had to sit down and wait until he could actually speak. They would occasionally meet when my father was out ploughing. But once they'd got over the initial bit of understanding why he had problems speaking when he came to the house, they actually quite liked him, they said he was just a polite man.[11]

Donald Ewen says that his father and Aunt Katie returned Orwell's politeness by refraining from speaking their native Gaelic in his company: 'My father and my Aunt Katie were both natural speakers but they probably wouldn't have spoken it in front of Orwell because here it was considered impolite and offensive to converse in Gaelic in front of a non-speaker.' Katie Darroch recalled Orwell being a cheery and happy visitor who would make himself at home and say: 'I can't resist your scones, Katie!'[12] Susan Watson long remembered the Darrochs as being kind and gentle neighbours.

For a man with a life-long prejudice against Scots, Orwell quickly developed a respect and sympathy for the islanders and showed a willingness to muck in when his health allowed it:

Thanks ever so for the tea – it came just at the right moment because this week the whole of the nearest village is being brought here in lorries to get in the field of corn in front of our house, and of course tea will have to flow like water while the job is on. We have been helping the crofter who is our only neighbour with his hay and corn, at least when rain hasn't made it impossible to work.[13]

His friend George Woodcock and has wife were confirmed coffee drinkers, and so saved their tea rations to send Orwell occasional packets of Typhoo, which made the dark, strong brew that he liked. For Woodcock, Orwell's tea-making for the harvesters 'reflected the intense interest he always took in in the concrete aspects of life – particularly rural life – and also in its social overtones'.[14] Orwell acutely observed and pondered the economic circumstances his neighbours found themselves in. He reported to Woodcock: 'The crofters have to work very hard, but in many ways they are better off and more independent than a town labourer, and they would be quite comfortable if they could get a bit of help in the way of machinery, electrical power and roads, and could get the landlords off their back and get rid of the deer. These animals are so common on this particular island that they are an absolute curse.'

Orwell's labours alongside the islanders didn't go unnoticed. Katie Darroch remembered: 'My brother Donald was very friendly with him. He was a good neighbour and would help you in any way he could. He was one of those who are willing to help anyone.'[15]

The self-reliant Orwell loved the spartan challenge of living at Barnhill, but his health wasn't up to it. Tosco Fyvel recalls Susan Watson telling him that Orwell worked himself into a state of exhaustion there, that he always felt the cold badly and would write in bed, sitting propped up against his old iron bedstead wearing 'an old, seedy dressing-gown with a frayed belt'. The atmosphere in his bedroom was thick and unhealthy due to a paraffin stove that gave off fumes and the fire grate which belched smoke and in which Orwell sometimes cured kippers.

Susan, who was half-Scottish but had never been there before, was thrilled by Jura, thinking it romantic and magical, but Orwell failed to inform her that Avril was already ensconced in Barnhill. Avril had little time for Susan and the feeling was reciprocated. They had first met at Canonbury Square. 'Immediately, we didn't like each other,' recorded Susan. 'It was nothing that either of us did. She looked at me with extreme disapproval. She was very sour.'

That summer, Orwell relished the outdoor life and the time he spent with his son. 'I have had several glorious months doing no work whatever,' he boasted in early August. Later that month he was supposed to travel to Glasgow to meet Susan Watson's daughter Sarah, who was arriving from London by train, and the challenges of island life are made clear in the problems he encountered on the way. Orwell began his journey on his motorbike but punctured a tyre on Jura's 'hell road'. He got a lift on a lorry and caught the ferry that crossed to neighbouring island of Islay where he hoped to catch a plane to Glasgow. The flight that day was full, so he took a bus to Port Ellen intending to take the 'steamer' to the mainland the following morning, but a cattle show meant that there wasn't a bed to be had there so he spent the night sharing a cell in the village police station with 'a lot of other people including a married couple with a perambulator'. He finally got to Glasgow, picked Sarah up and brought her home – walking the last five miles after the hire car from MacKechnie's shop in Craighouse had dropped them at the end of the drivable track. The next morning, he got a lift to where he had abandoned his motorbike, repaired the puncture and rode home where, that very day, he decided to buy a little boat with an outboard motor to make the journey from Barnhill to Craighouse easier, at least on calm days.

That summer the little Barnhill community was a fractious one. It may be that Avril believed that the live-in housekeeper had designs on her lonely brother, although the George/Susan relationship, while warm, was platonic and Tosco Fyvel thought Orwell treated her 'like a young sister looking after his infant'. Orwell was, nevertheless, desperately lonely, and any suspicions Avril may have had about Susan may have been due to over-protectiveness. In the tight little 'family' small things niggled. To Avril, her brother was 'Eric', but to Susan, he was 'George'. Susan also told radio producer Stephen Wadhams of CBC that Avril had said that Susan's disability made her unsuitable for island life, although she herself would later marry a farmer who had lost a leg. Biographer Jeffrey Meyers has harsh words for Avril, describing her as 'sour, spinsterish and resentful'.

Into this chilly atmosphere dropped the impoverished poet Paul Potts, a Soho habitué and close friend of Orwell's. The only thing that seems to have united Avril and Susan was their dislike of Potts, whose habits were bohemian and conversation unrestrained. Avril recalled to Bernard Crick that the eccentric Potts talked 'incessantly, frankly and freely on nothing but difficult or improper subjects'. Potts, in a misguided effort to make himself useful, infuriated people by cutting down and chopping up for firewood the only nut-bearing tree at Barnhill, along with trees that served as the exposed garden's windbreak. Potts recalled that Orwell himself was forgiving: 'Orwell took great care at dinner that night to be kind to me. I had extra roast beef.'[16]

In another incident guaranteed to raise the temperature, Susan used some scrap paper to light a fire. The 'scrap paper' turned out to be a novel that Potts was writing. Soon the poet abandoned the Barnhill salon in high dudgeon and was seen hiking off early one morning in the direction of Craighouse to catch the ferry to the mainland, his worldly possessions in a rucksack on his back. Potts and Orwell, however, remained close friends. 'I so resented these people who wasted Eric's time,' Avril told Bernard Crick in 1976. She was also annoyed when Inez Holden, a bohemian writer friend of Orwell's, came to stay and invented 'the silly game of shouting "Cannibals!" whenever strangers appeared'.

Sally McEwan and her young daughter also arrived at Barnhill for a visit. Sally had been Orwell's secretary at *Tribune* and had been his lover when he was married to Eileen. She was a strict vegetarian and her presence in Avril's kitchen – where rabbit, venison and seafood were staples – was not welcome. Avril recalled that hikers and yachtsmen would occasionally call at Barnhill, to the annoyance of her brother. Orwell, however, made locals welcome, offering tea and scones and something stronger if they had brought supplies or mail from Craighouse or Ardlussa.

The arrival of Susan Watson's boyfriend caused new tensions. David Holbrook was a bright and agreeable young man whose studies at Cambridge had been interrupted by service in a tank regiment in which he had served as a lieutenant during the D-Day landings. Holbrook went on to become a novelist, poet, critic and distinguished academic who wrote scores of books, and one can imagine the excitement with which the once-again-student must have travelled from Cambridge to Jura with offerings of food and an outboard motor for Orwell's boat. On the long journey he had doubtless imagined invigorating and intellectually stimulating walks on beautiful Jura and long fireside chats into the wee small hours about the state of British politics and literature with a distinguished novelist and journalist. Instead, he found unconcealed hostility towards him – right from the start. On the final hike up the track towards Barnhill Holbrook first encountered his host. 'There was this fellow shooting this goose! He was wearing sort of dismal oilskins, and he greeted me, shall we say, with suspicion and rather cold resentment. I think he thought I'd been sent by the Communist Party. He knew I was a Communist, or he'd gathered it, and was very much on his guard.'[17]

Like countless thousands of Britons, Holbrook had admired the Soviet Union, its leader Joseph Stalin and the blood sacrifice of the Red Army during the Second World War. Meanwhile Orwell was in his room delving deep into his memories of the NKVD purge in Barcelona – which had almost cost him and Eileen their liberty and very likely their lives – to write his warning to humankind. He had seen the results of the totalitarianism of both the left and right and he had no desire to share his writer's retreat with a follower of 'Uncle Joe'.

In 1976 Bernard Crick interviewed Holbrook, who told the biographer that he found both Orwell and his sister cold and morose. He showed Crick an early unpublished novel of his that featured thinly disguised and deeply unflattering portraits of George and Avril. Holbrook himself would appear in a novel by the poet Norman Bissell in which Orwell fears that the young communist is a spy who has been sent to kill him in a Trotsky-style assassination. In Bissell's *Barnhill* Orwell always carries a Luger pistol when Holbrook is around. 'You never know when you'll get a bullet in the back of the neck,' Bissell has Orwell musing.[18] Bissell was not the first writer to fictionalise Orwell's experience of Stalinism. American historian Thurston Clarke's novel spins a lively tale of a missing notebook of Orwell's that has the potential to unmask an American tech-millionaire and confident of the US President as being a Soviet spy and former Stalinist agent during the Spanish Civil War.[19] Susan Watson confirmed to Bernard Crick that Orwell did have a revolver on Jura, but the only record of him arming himself with it was when a bull was about to be loaded onto a lorry at Barnhill and Orwell feared that it might go on the rampage.

David Holbrook's novel not only savages the Blair siblings' characters but also disparages the fictionalised Avril's cooking, although other visitors recalled enjoying the meals she cooked, and Orwell's son Richard, who was brought up by Avril, remembers his aunt as a good cook, 'not fancy, but good'. Susan Watson recalled that every three weeks they killed and ate one of the domestic geese they raised and told of Avril sitting in the barn plucking the goose, 'looking witchlike'. Goose for dinner was a double treat for Susan as she thought they tasted 'gorgeous', and there was one less to terrify Richard and peck his bottom. 'They were noisy, filthy creatures,' she recalled. 'I was always slopping about in goose muck.' In late August that year Orwell complained in his diary: 'Geese got into the garden for only a few minutes & ate every lettuce to the ground.'

The following day Orwell went to help Donald Darroch gather in his hay: 'The midges were so bad as to make it almost impossible to work. Tried to help him, but driven out of the field after about half an hour. D. D. ditto. One is actually breathing them into one's nostrils, & the irritation is maddening. Forgot to mention I was yesterday stung by a wasp – almost the first I have seen this year.'

Orwell had always been a would-be craftsman – keen to work with his hands, if of limited skill. Friends remembered that the chairs he made were uncomfortable and that his bookcases sagged, but life on Jura meant that even his cack-handed efforts had their place. 'Well, he did settle down and do things for himself because you couldn't get a tradesman if you broke a window or a pipe burst,' Avril told Malcolm Muggeridge in an interview for the BBC. That self-reliance was an ingrained habit of Jura's people and Orwell carefully watched how Donald Darroch went about his croft-work, even writing detailed descriptions of how the crofter set and sharpened the blade on his scythe, and he did drawings in his diary to illustrate the techniques. He was keen to take Darroch's advice. 'Tried scythe,' he wrote. 'With it as it is now, I can get a little grass off, & might improve with practice.'

Donald Darroch was something of a role model for the aspiring Hebridean smallholder, and Orwell watched him skin a deer carcass they were to share and pickle in brine for the winter.

This close association with the lives of the down-to-earth folk of Jura was a new experience for the forty-three-year-old writer. He was witnessing a community that had adapted itself to the challenges of its environment and circumstances, much in the way the mining communities he had explored when writing *The Road to Wigan Pier* had adapted to their harsh lot. On Jura, the sweat broken by the local crofters and farm workers may have been the first honest sweat he had ever seen broken by Scotsmen, and a far cry from the whisky-tainted perspiration leaking from Scots bent over the billiard tables of the whites-only clubs of imperial Burma.

Normally all the adults in the house ate together in the kitchen but on one occasion that David Holbrook recalled, Orwell became 'all Burma Police' when 'the laird' arrived at Barnhill with a shooting party, and the author and Avril entertained the party in sitting room while Holbrook and Susan had tea with the beaters in the kitchen, in the manner of *Upstairs Downstairs*. Biographer Jeffrey Meyers tartly commented: 'Some visitors, quite clearly, were more equal than others.'[20] Holbrook said that he and Susan developed a very jokey, self-protecting ironic attitude to Orwell and Avril and that he was certain that the writer suspected they were taking the mickey out of him. Holbrook also revealed to CBC that he and Susan used to sneak into Orwell's writing room and take peeks at his manuscript. They found it 'pretty depressing stuff' with 'dismal sexual episodes' and 'depressingly lacking in hope'. For Holbrook, the end of war, a progressive social programme and a flourishing new theatre scene were portents of a better future, not a grim dystopian one. He later commented:

That was what was so strange by contrast, to go into this remoteness and find this man expressing a loss of hope for the future of the world. A man who was ill, rather grumpy, and had altogether fled the world because he feared atomic war, and there with his sister, who was a very dismal woman. It was disturbing to see this man shrinking away from humanity and pouring out all this very bitter hopelessness.[21]

The emotional storm cloud gathering over Barnhill soon burst and Susan, Sarah and Holbrook left suddenly after a row, carrying their possessions to Ardlussa seven miles away, an arduous journey over rough track, especially for Susan who was not fully mobile. Margaret Fletcher remembered them arriving, very wet, at her doorstep one evening as it was getting dark. 'Susan was in a state of exhaustion,' she said. 'We put them up and they left the next day by the post bus.' The lack of a lift from Barnhill, however, was not an act of spite. Orwell simply hadn't a vehicle at that time. Richard missed Susan terribly. Katie Darroch remembered: 'The poor wee laddie, he cried and cried.'[22] David Holbrook's 1983 interview with Stephen Wadhams clearly shows that Orwell and Avril were unforgiven for the 'shattering' experience he had had at Barnhill, but the rows and dramatic departure seem to have caused no long-standing ill-will between Susan and her employer. When interviewed for the five-part BBC *Arena* series that transmitted in late 1983, Susan spoke warmly of him. Her daughter Sarah told biographer D.J. Taylor that her mother's year with Orwell on Jura was the happiest of her life.

There is no doubt that Orwell and his sister gave Susan's intelligent boyfriend the cold shoulder. For Orwell, it might have been Holbrook's communism; for Avril, his attachment to Susan; but biographer Richard Bradford postulates that in alienating himself on a remote island where conventions of sociability didn't rule as they did in London, previously unnoticed elements of Orwell's character came to the surface.[23] Avril, who had now built her life around her brother, may have taken the lead from Orwell's hostility.

While David Holbrook was scathing about the 'dismal' Avril Blair, Margaret Fletcher had only praise for her:

> She was an exceptional person. She was 41 when she came and had an interesting and varied life. We quickly became friends. One of her great gifts was to be able to see the amusing side of the many problems at Barnhill.
>
> Maybe the house wasn't very tidy, but at least everybody had good meals. She did what she could to make sure everybody was looked after. There was always a pot of tea, and she was a very good baker and an admirable housekeeper.[24]

Richard Blair regrets that his aunt Avril has been side-lined by his father's biographers and at a meeting of the Orwell Society paid tribute to her devotion to his father and her efforts at Barnhill:

> She was absolutely crucial to his existence at Barnhill. Without her he wouldn't have managed. There's no question about it. Much as he thought he could have managed without her he would have been lost. She had a very good relationship with her brother they were very close, as close as families of those days were. The middle class didn't show their emotions terribly much. Not a lot of hugging and kissing went on. She was devoted to him, and he to her. No question about it. So there was a really good relationship between the two of them and she has been side-lined by biographers and that ought to be put right.

At Barnhill, Avril liberated her brother to do what he did best. Since his decision almost twenty years earlier to resign from the Burma police and become a writer he had driven himself relentlessly.

He felt compelled to write every day, believing that a day without writing was a day wasted. On Jura he was writing this thirteenth book and also penned scores of reviews, essays and columns. Fed, watered and generally cared for by Avril, he was at last free to summon all the remaining strength he had to write his final work.

But dedication to his craft did not blind him to his surroundings. Orwell's diary for July 1946 is crammed with accounts of his gardening and fishing efforts, weather records and wildlife observations: 'Another spotted orchid is coming up, this time a dark mauve one'; 'Stags now have very large horns, but still velvety'; 'Terns very busy & noisy over the little island at the mouth of the harbour at Kinuachdrach'. On 21 July he complained of 'miserable weather … cold enough to make one want a fire in every room'. Ten days later he noted: 'Beautiful fine day, & quite hot.' He records making a handle for a sledgehammer from a bough of mountain ash, and he carefully observed and wrote about Donald and Katie Darroch's technique for tending their quarter-acre turnip field: 'D.D. will not use a hoe as he says that if one does one cannot single out the strongest plants.' It is a diary of a fulfilling month, rich in action and observation.

In late August *Animal Farm* was published in America and was then quickly re-released by the American Book of the Month Club with sales of half a million copies. For the first time since he had left the Burma police, the wolf had stalked away from Orwell's door and he was able to give up much of his journalism, although he did resume his *As I Please* column for *Tribune*. By September Jura was beginning to show how challenging it could be. Mid-month Orwell reported that torrential rain had made the track to Ardlussa a running stream, in some places two feet deep. To collect their weekly rations meant a two-hour journey on bicycles, and a three-hour return journey when laden. On 13 October Orwell's boat dragged her anchor in a storm and three of its boards were staved in. Three days later ten or twenty people turned up at Kinauchdrachd to help Donald Darroch harvest his field of oats, but the driving rain made the operation a shambles. Orwell's diary of this period is littered with the phrases 'awful day', 'dreadful day', 'vile day' and 'wind raging all night'. As temperatures fell, Orwell recorded the amount of Calor gas, paraffin and coal the family was using up in order to make life bearable.

In early October Orwell drew diagrams of his garden showing his plans for it and planning his crop rotation for 1947 and '48. He also compiled a 'things to do' list and a shopping list of necessities to get for the house including, rugs, carpets, chairs, various tools and a radio. On the eighth of that month, a fine dry day but cold and windy, Orwell noted, 'Garden is now finished, i.e., is up to schedule.' The following day the family left for London.

Orwell spent the wicked winter of 1946/47 in London and revealed to Tosco Fyvel that the bitterly cold weather had further damaged his health. In January, England experienced temperatures as low as −21°C (−6°F), and February was one of the coldest months on record. At Kew Gardens no sunshine was recorded for twenty days in February and the temperature never rose above 5°C (41°F) that month. In contrast, the west of Scotland was mostly dry and sunny although very cold. The situation in London was made worse by coal and food shortages as transport was disrupted and vegetables froze in the ground. March brought blizzards and then flooding. In London people scavenged bombed-out buildings for timber to burn and Orwell himself chopped an old bedstead and some wooden toys he had made for his son into firewood. Richard Blair has early memories of that flat, and one of them is of being cold.[25] Tosco Fyvel visited Orwell that winter, finding the writer alone as Avril was out with Richard, and remembered that Orwell was seriously ill with bronchitis but still rising from his bed to write.

Despite the severity of that winter, Orwell returned alone to Jura in the last days of December to plant fruit trees and roses bushes. He arrived on 2 January 1947.

Was due to arrive two days earlier, but missed the boat on 30th & had to spend about 2 days in Glasgow. Rough crossing from Tarbert, & was very sick. Did not take tablets until on the point of being sick – on the return journey shall take them before embarking. It took the boat about half an hour to tie up at Craighouse pier, as with the sea that was running she could not get in close. After tying up she could only keep in position for a minute or two, in spite of the cables, & the passengers had only just time to nip across the gangway.[26]

The day he arrived had been stormy but beautifully sunny. The following morning the storm increased, and Orwell wrote that the wind was so violent that it was hard to stay on his feet. Barnhill, left unheated, must have been freezing, but Orwell makes no complaint about that in his diary, although laments that rabbits had eaten his cabbages and turnips and destroyed most of his strawberries. Undeterred, he planted red and black currant bushes, gooseberries, rhubarb, raspberries and roses and set traps for rabbits. He recorded that he had about a two-month supply of paraffin, coal and Calor gas ready for when he returned.

By 9 January, Orwell was back in Islington in time to hear the BBC Third Programme's adaptation of *Animal Farm*. But had he really left Jura behind? The island, and what he thought and felt abouts its people were never far from his active, inquisitive mind.

CHAPTER 8

Scotland's Case Against England

'Stands Scotland where she did?'
'Alas, poor country, almost afraid to know itself.'

—William Shakespeare, *The Tragedy of Macbeth*,
1606

In London in early 1947, and doubtless reflecting on his experiences on Jura, Orwell wrote an *As I Please* column for *Tribune* in which he discussed the Gaelic language he had heard spoken around him on Jura.

> At one time I would have said that it is absurd to keep alive an archaic language like Gaelic, spoken by only a few hundred thousand people. Now I am not so sure. To begin with, if people feel that they have a special culture which ought to be preserved, and that the language is part of it, difficulties should not be put in their way when they want their children to learn it properly. Secondly, it is probable that the effort of being bilingual is a valuable education in itself. The Scottish Gaelic-speaking peasants speak beautiful English, partly, I think, because English is an almost foreign language which they sometimes do not use for days together. Probably they benefit intellectually by having to be aware of dictionaries and grammatical rules, as their English opposite numbers would not be.[1]

For the first time in his life Orwell had begun to seriously regard a part of Britain that was not England.

*

The royal coat of arms of the United Kingdom features a lion and a unicorn. With the lion representing England, and the unicorn Scotland, they symbolise the Union of the Crowns in 1603 when James VI of Scotland ascended to the English throne as James I. This United Kingdom, strengthened a little over a century later by the union of the Scots and English parliaments, is almost entirely ignored in *The Lion and the Unicorn*, the short book Orwell wrote during the Second World War to point the country in a new and more progressive direction and towards a socialist revolution. The clue to this omission is in the book's secondary title: *Socialism and the English Genius*. The work, like most of Orwell's hundreds of essays, letters, articles and novels, is about England – almost entirely about England, as if Scotland, Wales and Northern Ireland were not also at war against Nazi Germany and had no stake in the outcome of that conflict or right to re-order their societies in the wake of it. Orwell, no royalist (although his strategy for 'an English revolution' did *not* including abolishing the monarchy) might be forgiven for not being acquainted with the arcane imagery of heraldry, but such a misjudged title for a book that simply ignored three of the four nations of the United Kingdom is indicative of Orwell's hitherto narrowly English-centric view of Britain.

Throughout his writing life Orwell habitually ignored Scotland, Wales and Northern Ireland. If he mentioned Scotland and Ireland at all, he showed 'deplorable prejudice' towards both and failed 'to consider how much English character has been shaped by the multi-national culture and politics of the United Kingdom'.[2]

The scholar and Orwell biographer Richard Bradford says that in *The Lion and Unicorn* Orwell 'tries to tie down the true nature of what it means to be English, without entirely excluding the Scots and the Welsh'. I disagree. Orwell *almost* entirely excludes the Scots and the Welsh and merely offers the oft-heard lame excuse that the word 'England' actually means 'Britain', as if ignoring three out of Britain's four nations is merely a slip of the tongue. In fact, all the examples of national character he refers to in the essay (UK Labour Exchanges apart) are English: 'The clatter of clogs in the Lancashire mill towns, the to-and-fro of the lorries on the Great North Road, the queues outside the Labour Exchanges, the rattle of pin-tables in the Soho pubs, the old maids biking to Holy Communion through the mists of the autumn morning …' There are no striking Tonypandy miners facing down armed troops, no Red Clydesiders agitating for revolution, no sons of Ulster marching towards the Somme and not even a folksy welcome in the valleys or thrifty and thirsty Jocks. Here is Orwell's entire section in the book that refers to Scotland and Wales:

And even Welsh and Scottish readers are likely to have been offended because I have used the word 'England' oftener than 'Britain', as though the whole population dwelt in London and the Home Counties and neither north nor west possessed a culture of its own.

One gets a better view of this question if one considers the minor point first. It is quite true that the so-called races of Britain feel themselves to be very different from one another. A Scotsman, for instance, does not thank you if you call him an Englishman. You can see the hesitation we feel on this point by the fact that we call our islands by no less than six different names, England, Britain, Great Britain, the British Isles, the United Kingdom and, in very exalted moments, Albion.

Apart from these 134 words, the 23,000-word book could be the manifesto for a revolution in the independent nation state of England. Scotland's unicorn is redundant. The red dragon of Wales doesn't even get a look in. There are no red hands or shamrocks.

Even though Orwell believed that England was a family 'with the wrong members in control', he was self-consciously and patriotically English and had great difficulty in seeing the United Kingdom of Great Britain and Northern Ireland as anything but 'England'. Christopher Hitchens maintained that Orwell 'was something of a sceptic about Britishness and Union'. And Stephen Spender argued that Orwell fitted into a very distinct form of radical Conservativism that stretched back to the nineteenth century and people like William Cobbett: 'What he valued was the old concept of England based on the English countryside, in which to be conservative is to be against change taking place, especially changes in the direction of producing inequality. He was opposed to the whole hard-faced industrial middle class which arose in the nineteenth century.'[3]

As for Orwell's claim that 'we call our islands by no less than six different names', that may be true of himself and some English folk, but most of us UK citizens living outside England don't. To Scots, Welsh and Northern Irish, and to an increasing number of English people, England is England and not a catch-all name for the archipelago (the Irish Republic excluded) off the western coast of Europe. Simply by claiming that he inaccurately described Britain as England does not mean that Orwell did not choose to ignore, or was simply ignorant of, matters west of Offa's Dyke or north of Hadrian's Wall. To him, England was the part that mattered. Until Orwell moved to Jura towards the end of his life, the Celtic fringes were simply add-ons of such little significance that they need scarcely be mentioned because the views, cultures and customs of these areas need not be considered.

The German Luftwaffe had paid tribute to Scotland's heavy industrial might during the Second World War with raids on Clydebank, Glasgow, Greenock, Edinburgh, Aberdeen and Dundee, yet when Orwell describes the 'the old-style "proletarian"

– collarless, unshaven and with muscles warped by heavy labour …' he reports that such men exist only 'in the heavy-industry areas of the north of England'. But in 1941 the vast majority of Scots belonged to the working class, many of them employed in the coal, steel, engineering and shipbuilding industries, and yet their labours are unworthy of mention. This is highly unlikely to be a deliberate slight, but it shows that Orwell had a blind spot for even the Socialist-minded parts of Britain outside England. They were communities whose existence he scarcely acknowledged existed. And while he admired (perhaps even idolised) the miners he encountered while researching *The Road to Wigan Pier*, the miners of Scotland and Wales who also fuelled the fires of Britain's war effort were invisible to him. If Orwell had fought in Spain alongside such Brigadistas as George Smith, a miner from Methil in Fife who had been 'out' in the 1926 miners' strike; Archibald Dewar, an Aberdeen blacksmith who was probably captured and executed by Franco's men; hunger-marcher Joseph 'Jock' Cunningham of Glasgow or Roddy MacFarquhar, an Inverness railway booking clerk who I myself had the honour of knowing in his later years; he might have developed the understanding and admiration for working class and radical Scots as he did for his Catalan comrades.[4]

Orwell's view of the state he belonged to is even more Anglo-dominated when, in exalted language, he calls for the 'revolution that the native genius of the English people' will bring about: 'The Stock Exchange will be pulled down, the horse plough will give way to the tractor, the country houses will be turned into children's holiday camps, the Eton and Harrow match will be forgotten, but England will still be England, an everlasting animal stretching into the future and the past …'

He is talking here of a deep atavistic English spirit that recalls G.K. Chesterton's 'For we are the people of England, that never have spoken yet'. His rhetoric becomes positively Churchillian when summing up his essay: 'We must add to our heritage or lose it, we must grow greater or grow less, we must go forward or backward. I believe in England, and I believe that we shall go forward.'

It was the United Kingdom that faced Nazi invasion when Orwell wrote these words in very early 1941, not England, and presumably Orwell wished his revolution to succeed in the other nations of the United Kingdom as well as England. And yet, time and again, Orwell used the term 'England' not 'Britain'. This cannot be lazy nomenclature; Orwell was not that kind of writer. For all his deeply held socialist beliefs, the lower-upper-middle-class Old Etonian from an empire-serving family was hard-wired to an emotional and political Englishness which had little or no understanding of, or respect for, the three other British nations.

Orwell had only the vaguest notion of Scottish geography. Once, while travelling on a train south from Glasgow with Richard Rees, they had just cleared the suburbs of Glasgow when Orwell commented: 'The weather seems just the same in England,' in the belief that England began immediately south of Glasgow, not sixty miles further south. 'At first,' remembered Rees, 'he couldn't understand my surprise, but he became more interested when I gave the matter a literary slant by pointing out that the part of Scotland whose existence he ignored included the birthplace of Carlyle, the Burns country and the Walter Scott country.'

Orwell consistently underestimated the patriotism felt in the smaller nations, arguing in *The Lion and the Unicorn* that national differences within the UK 'fade away' when viewed by a foreigner who might be hard put to recognise the difference between Brits of the four nations, and that this tourist myopia proved that they belonged to a single civilisation. But the necessary broad-brush and superficial view of the foreigner is hardly the gauge with which to measure national identity and nationhood.

Scotland's Case Against England

*

On Jura Orwell began to see things differently – and to argue with his own prejudices. It was at this time that he wrote an article that established him as probably the first English political thinker of his generation to understand Scottish resentment at Westminster's neglectful high-handedness, and that Scottish national sentiment – nurtured by its own history, church and educational and legal systems – was beginning to seep into the politics of that ancient nation. He was witnessing the long, slow progress of Scottish nationalism, and he was hard-wired to dislike what he saw.

Having endured wars in which nationalism and fascism had marched in step, Orwell was deeply troubled by the connection. In *Tribune*, his *As I Please* column posed the question: *What is Fascism?* It was a term that he felt had become 'almost meaningless' in the way it was used, with Orwell maintaining: 'There is almost no set of people – certainty no political party or organised body of any kind – which has not been denounced as Fascist during the past ten years.' Among those dubbed 'fascist' were nationalists. He wrote: 'Nationalism is universally regarded as inherently Fascist, but this is held only to apply to such national movements as the speaker happens to disapprove of: Arab nationalism, Polish nationalism, Finnish nationalism, The Indian Congress Party, the Muslim League, Zionism and the I.R.A. are all described as Fascist – but not by the same people.'[5]

Claiming that 'I am a patriot, but you are a nasty nationalist' is an easy trap to fall into. To cut through the name-calling, Orwell sought to define what he meant by 'nationalism':

By Nationalism I mean first of all the habit of assuming that human beings can be classified like insects and that whole blocks of millions or tens of millions of people can be

119

confidently labelled 'good' or 'bad'. But secondly – and this is much more important – I mean the habit of identifying oneself with a single nation or other unit. Nationalism is not to be confused with patriotism. Both words are normally used in so vague a way that any definition is liable to be challenged, but one must draw a distinction between them, since two different and even opposing ideas are involved. By 'patriotism' I mean devotion to a particular place and a particular way of life, which one believes to be the best in the world but has no wish to force upon other people. Patriotism is of its nature defensive, both militarily and culturally. Nationalism, on the other hand, is inseparable from the desire for power. The abiding purpose of every nationalist is to secure more power and more prestige, not for himself but for the nation or other unit in which he has chosen to sink his own individuality.[6]

In *Burmese Days* Orwell had denounced imperialism through his protagonist John Flory. A teak planter and pukka sahib of fifteen years, Flory lamented: 'Year after year you sit in Kipling-haunted little Clubs, whisky to right of you, Pink'un to left of you, listening and eagerly agreeing while Colonel Bodger develops his theory that these bloody Nationalists should be boiled in oil.'

Orwell's Burmese 'anti-imperialists' seeking freedom from British rule were Colonel Bodger's 'bloody nationalists', deserving to be boiled in oil. Were these Burmese students and young Buddhist monks patriotic freedom fighters or fascist nationalists? The abiding purpose of the great nationalist movements that sprang up or reached their zenith throughout the colonies of the British Empire after the Second World War was to achieve self-determination, with no desire to force a way of life on other peoples. '*Sinn Féin Amháin*' (Ourselves Alone) was the creed of the Irish nationalists, but the Gaelic phrase doubtless had its equivalents throughout Africa, the East and Caribbean. Could Orwell realistically have argued that fascism was the blood-brother of nationalism to an Irish Nationalist or an Indian Nationalist (with whom Orwell overtly sympathised)? The great critic William Empson worked in the same BBC department during the war as Orwell and recalled: 'George was intensely devoted to the liberation of India ... so much so that he felt Hitler's war would be worth it if it spelled the end of the British Raj, as it was likely to do if properly handled.'[7] David Astor concurred: 'He wanted to do things like work for the independence of India during the war, because he thought that a war against oppression and racialism must include a change in the British attitude towards India, or a speeding up of the self-government of India.'[8]

However, unlike the progressive nationalism – or patriotism – that would make India independent in 1947, Burma the following year, and set free more than a score of other British colonies on three continents by 1967, Celtic nationalism, in Orwell's mind, was rooted in regressive and racist ideology:

Welsh, Irish and Scottish nationalism have points of difference but are alike in their anti-English orientation. Members of all three movements have opposed the war while continuing to describe themselves as pro-Russian, and the lunatic fringe has even contrived to be simultaneously pro-Russian and pro-Nazi. But Celtic nationalism is not the same thing as Anglophobia. Its motive force is a belief in the past and future greatness of the Celtic peoples, and has a strong tinge of racialism. The Celt is supposed to be spiritually superior to the Saxon – simpler, more creative, less vulgar, less snobbish, etc. – but the usual power-hunger is there under the surface. One symptom of it is the delusion that Eire, Scotland or even Wales could preserve its independence unaided and owes nothing to British protection.

Among writers, good examples of this school of thought are Hugh MacDiarmid and Sean O'Casey. No modern Irish writer, even of the stature of Yeats or Joyce, is completely free from traces of nationalism.[9]

Orwell was, however, unable to judge those who wrote in Irish or Scots Gaelic, or in Welsh. Neither could Orwell have anticipated the future prosperity of an Ireland within the European Union, or the centre-left social-democratic position of the SNP, which at the time of writing has been the elected governing party in Scotland's parliament for fifteen years. Nor could he see that rather than placing your own country 'beyond good and evil and recognising no other duty than that of advancing its interests', many small nation states that were not previously independent – the Republic of Ireland, Norway, Estonia, Iceland and New Zealand, for instance – are resolutely internationalist in their outlook, playing significant roles in bodies like the EU, EFTA, NATO and the UN. But while Orwell did not foresee what progressive 'patriotic' nationalism might look like, he was prescient enough to recognise that discontent over the governance of Scotland might put Scots on a home-rule – or nationalist – trajectory.

Early in 1947, probably in London and not long back from Jura, Orwell penned one of his regular *As I Please* columns for *Tribune* in which, for the first time in his career, he looked seriously at Scottish identity and the emergence of Scottish nationalism. It was prompted by a letter from someone he describes as a 'Scottish Nationalist' but does not identify. Arguing that the end-of-war Yalta agreement had betrayed Poland and that Polish ex-soldiers had been 'cast aside and dumped in Scotland', the letter writer argued that 'Scotland experienced her Yalta in 1707 when English gold achieved what English guns could not do'.[10]

Scotland's Case Against England

Orwell concluded that 'the writer hates us as bitterly as a devout Nazi would hate a Jew'. It may well be that the letter writer was an anti-English bigot but, instead of merely tossing the rant into the bin, Orwell used it as a catalyst to consider the potential for a resurgent Scottish nationalism – and he did so with more understanding that might have been expected from a lifelong Scotophobe. He was almost certainly the first English political thinker to recognise that what had hitherto been a more literary movement than a political one had the potential to grow into a broad civil movement. While Orwell is tagged as 'prescient' in foreseeing the surveillance society and the rise of fake news, he is little credited with recognising the root causes of a movement that would come to dominate Scottish politics and challenge the unity of the British state:

> In this country I don't think it is enough realized – I myself had no idea of it until a few years ago – that Scotland has a case against England. On economic grounds it may not be a very strong case. In the past, certainly, we have plundered Scotland shamefully, but whether it is *now* true that England as a whole exploits Scotland as a whole, and that Scotland would be better off if fully autonomous, is another question. The point is that many Scottish people, often quite moderate in outlook, are beginning to think about autonomy and to feel that they are pushed into an inferior position. They have a good deal of reason. In some areas, at any rate, Scotland is almost an occupied country. You have an English or anglicized upper class, and a Scottish working class which speaks with a markedly different accent, or even, part of the time, in a different language.[11]

Orwell's insistence that Scottish nationalism had the potential to grow defied the imagination of English politicos. A solitary

SNP MP was elected in the Motherwell by-election of 1945, during a wartime truce under which the major parties did not contest elections, but the seat was lost soon after in the post-war election, and the history of the SNP in the 1940s and '50s is a catalogue of broken dreams and lost deposits. But the heather was smouldering. The non-party Scottish Covenant Association collected nearly two million signatures in favour of a degree of home rule for Scotland, and many Scots were gleeful when four student 'Covenanters' broke into Westminster Abbey on Christmas day 1950 to 'recover' the Stone of Destiny and return it to Scotland from where it had been plundered by Edward I in 1296. A student jape rather than serious politics, certainly – but one applauded by many Scots who felt their country ignored and neglected by Westminster. They were, in Orwell's words, 'beginning to think about autonomy'. Orwell certainly could not have foreseen the North Sea oil and gas boom that began in the 1960s, peaked at the end of the century and fuelled dreams of independence, but he didn't need to witness the 'It's Scotland's Oil' campaign of the 1970s to recognise that many Scots might come to embrace a belief in either a degree of home rule or full independence.

To Orwell – deeply influenced by the era of imperialism, fascism and Stalinism – Scottish nationalism 'might develop in an ugly way, and the fact that there was a progressive Labour Government in London might not make much difference'. That Scottish nationalism was still just a fringe movement when Orwell wrote that, only prompted him to warn that 'the Communist Manifesto was once a very obscure document, and the Nazi party only had six members when Hitler joined it'. For Orwell, there was only one direction that a nationalist movement could go – the path to totalitarianism. But, as Orwell had pointed out, Scotland had been 'plundered shamefully' by England and was 'almost an occupied country'. In that case, wasn't seeking independence a 'patriotic' cause rather than a 'nationalist' one? England and the rest of Britain had almost become an occupied country in 1940 and would have been plundered shamefully by Nazi Germany. Orwell's response to that threat had been to agitate for patriotic resistance. 'Patriotism is of its nature defensive,' he had written.

Orwell's notion of nationalism did not, could not, anticipate that of the Scottish independence movement of the late twentieth and early twenty-first centuries. The civic nationalism of today's Scottish independence movement is nothing like that which Orwell feared. While the poet Hugh MacDiarmid listed his hobby as 'anglophobia', even a hardline Scottish nationalist like him had no desire for territorial expansion or power over other peoples, as his 1931 poem 'The Little White Rose' makes clear:

The rose of all the world is not for me.
I want for my part
Only the little white rose of Scotland
That smells sharp and sweet—and breaks the heart.[12]

So, no planned Scottish annexation of Berwick-upon-Tweed. No hunger for *Lebensraum* in Cumbria. No Black Watch assault craft on the beaches of the Isle of Man.

Even in Orwell's lifetime, progressive narratives of Scottish nationalism were available, if he had only read what radical pro-independence Scots were writing. As early as 1931 Robert Cunninghame Graham, who had been president of the first Labour Party in Britain (the Scottish Labour Party, which he co-founded with Keir Hardy) and later became president of the SNP, argued: 'Nationalism is the first step to the International goal which every thinking man and woman must place before their eyes but without Nationalism we cannot have any true Internationalism.'[13] Compared to Cunninghame Grahame, Orwell was a latecomer to the cause of anti-imperialism. In his maiden speech to the House of Commons, on 1 February 1887, Cunninghame Grahame had condemned the brutality with which Britain dealt with Burmese dissidents and, in an essay written seven years before Orwell's birth, the Scot lambasted the European entrepreneurs, adventurers and chancers who had carved up Africa on the British Empire's behalf: 'War club, assegai and boomerang, bolas, parang and krise, even if wielded by thousands avail but little against quick-firing guns. In stern reality the "native" is the hero, and the European "conquistador," as Beit, Barney Barnato, Selous, Rhodes & Co., nothing but cowardly interlopers, presuming on superior arms.'[14]

Graham railed against the inhumanity of British exploitation of its empire in Africa in a vigorous prose style worthy of Orwell himself, protesting that Africans 'without cannons have no rights. Their land is ours, their cattle and their fields, their houses ours; their arms, their poor utensils, and everything they have; their women too, are ours to use as concubines, to beat, exchange, to barter off for gunpowder or gin, ours to infect with syphilis, leave with child, outrage, torment, and make by contact with the vilest of our vile, more vile than beasts.'[15]

Orwell could never have foreseen that, far from being what Prime Minister Harold Wilson called 'the natural party of government', Labour would stall, slide and then descend into the freefall that saw the collapse of Labour's 'red wall' of constituencies in the north of England and the Conservative's eighty-seat majority in the 2019 UK General Election. Nor could he imagine the Labour Party in Scotland being outflanked on the left by the SNP (which Labour once derided as 'Tartan Tories') and withering away from 2007 at the end of Tony Blair's premiership. The Scottish voters – disillusioned with returning Labour MPs and getting Tory governments – switched to the party that Orwell rightly foresaw had the potential to grow, even though he had not anticipated that it would have evolved as a progressive party of the democratic cen-tre-left. What would he have made of the Scottish political theorist Tom Nairn's assertion that civic and secular nationalism would be an outward-looking and modernising force that would bring about the break-up of post-imperial Britain?[16] Would Orwell, if alive today, have sided with English journalist and Labour Party member Paul Mason when he said: 'I wish my party, Labour, would begin to accept and prepare itself for the very exciting prospect of a socialist republic of Scotland'?[17] Orwell supported Indian independence – so who knows?

While Orwell believed that Scotland's post-war ills would have to be cured alongside England's, he did recommend 'one small but not negligible point' that he believed would ease tensions. Living on Jura, the great English wordsmith had begun to recognise the value of the Gaelic he heard on a regular basis and realised that the lack of it in Gaeltacht schools caused resentment. Living among Gaels, wit-nessing their lives and respecting their community, he had come to respect their language. He complained about the paucity of broad-casts in Gaelic – only two or three half-hour programmes a week. These included a Friday evening news programme in the graveyard slot of 10.45 p.m. and Gaelic church services. The former BBC radio talks producer also thought that these broadcasts were 'rather ama-teurish' and suggested that there should be at least a daily Gaelic programme. It's quite a thought – George Orwell in the kitchen at Barnhill enjoying his nightly shot of rum or brandy while listening to the news in Gaelic after a hard day's writing. It's tempting to think that had he lived longer he might even have picked up some of the language. His son Richard points out that his father was a linguist who had learned several dialects of Burmese, spoke fluent French, could speak reasonable Spanish and probably Catalan.[18] Learning Gaelic was certainly within Orwell's capability – even if the time he had left to acquire it was not.

Did Orwell know he was on borrowed time? Could he have moved somewhere more conducive to his health? What we are certain of is that he was determined to return to Jura for what was to be one of the most critical periods of his writing life.

CHAPTER 9

Barnhill: All but Drowned

'In less than a second, you could get from this world into the next.'

—Emeric Pressburger's script, *I Know Where I'm Going!*
1945

On 11 April 1947 Orwell returned to Barnhill with his son and sister Avril. On this occasion, haven taken the London-to-Glasgow sleeper, they flew from Glasgow to Islay and then made the short ferry crossing from Port Askaig to Jura. 'I think it's really better,' he wrote. 'It costs £2 or £3 more, but it saves about 5 hours & the boredom of going on boats, & even if one was sick it's only three quarters of an hour whereas if one goes by sea one is sick for five or six hours, i.e. if it is bad weather.' Orwell was in poor shape, having been ill in bed the entire previous week, but the call of Jura was strong. His intention was clear – despite the island's isolation and lack of sophisticated medical facilities it was to be his permanent home, from which he would only make occasional sorties to London.

The day after he arrived at Barnhill he wrote by hand, 'because the typewriter is downstairs', a long letter to 'Dearest Sonia' Brownell with whom he had a brief affair and was almost certainly in love with. He described 'lovely spring weather' with 'daffodils all over the place', and while admitting that it had been 'a nightmare all today getting things straight' he said Barnhill was 'beginning to look quite civilised' and described the room she would have if she came to stay. He then goes to some length describing how she should travel to Jura and warns her to bring stout boots or gum boots. 'I do so want to have you here,' he almost pleads. 'Do come,

& come whenever you like for as long as you like, only try to let me know beforehand. And meanwhile take care of yourself & be happy.' He signs off: 'With much love George.'

Orwell relished the challenge of being self-reliant of Jura, but he was a desperately lonely man who longed for a woman to share his life and care for him and his son. That woman would not be Sonia Brownell. Although she eventually married her ailing suitor, she never visited him on Jura, and only ever went to Barnhill the month after he died.

All that spring Orwell the writer competed with Orwell the gardener and smallholder. Donald Darroch ploughed over an area of land in front of Barnhill where Orwell could grow potatoes and vegetables and build a hen house. Observing the strength of the south and west winds, he noted in his diary that it 'will need a lot of strengthening & weighting down to make it stay in place'. Clearly he underestimated the winds, for a week later the hen house was blown off its base in a 'very violent gale' and had to be lifted onto the base again, with the help of local men Duggie Clark and Neal MacArthur, and tied down with guy ropes.

Richard, frustrated by the winter-long restrictions of the London flat, enjoyed running free, but withing three days of arriving at Barnhill fell and gashed his forehead 'extremely badly' while standing on a chair watching his father making him a wooden toy. Richard recalled: 'There was consternation and there was blood and tears and I was bawling my head off and was carted off to the bathroom with blood streaming from my head ... I still have the scar. It runs across my forehead down to above my eye. I was stood by the sink and bled profusely.'[1]

The island's doctor lived in Craighouse twenty-five miles away and, due to lack of transport, Richard had to wait until the following day to be stitched up. Margaret Fletcher recalls holding the child as the doctor stitched while 'Eric looked miserably unhappy and occasionally came into the bathroom to see how we were getting on'.

Avril, too, suffered the consequence of living far from medical help. Dislocating her shoulder, she was taken in terrible pain to Ardlussa to see the doctor who had travelled up from Craighouse. He was unable to put her shoulder back in, so Avril had to be taken on a hazardous voyage to Crinan on the mainland in a tiny motorboat for treatment by a doctor from Lochgilphead. The weather was bad and, according to Orwell, she 'nearly drowned' on the way.

Richard Blair remembers a humorous and self-inflicted ailment. Finding an old pipe, he filled it with the cigarette dog-ends that his father had tossed into the fireplace: 'I then asked for a lighter and my father, without a break in the conversation, produced a lighter, handed it down behind the chair and I'd try and light this pipe. I thought: "They don't seem to know what I'm doing, they can't see me." So I lit this pipe with the inevitable consequences of course. Violently ill. This put me off smoking at least until I got to school.'

Ricky – as he was called – loved living at Barnhill and the freedom it gave him to roam around. He remembers going out fishing for lobsters and both his father and Avril reading to him, Beatrix Potter being a favourite. Orwell feared Richard might get bitten by adders, which are numerous on Jura and would slither into the Barnhill garden. 'Resolved to kill all snakes close to the house to be on the safe side with R[ichard],' he wrote in his diary. 'In killing it, cut it in half. Then picked up, as I thought, the safe end to examine it, but it was the head, which promptly tried to bite me.' There are accounts of him ruthlessly killing any snake he encountered, on one occasion standing on the snake's head and eviscerating it with his penknife. 'It surprised me terribly because he always struck me as being very gentle to animals,' said Bill Dunn, who witnessed the slaughter. 'My father was concerned about snakes,' Richard told the Orwell Society. 'Not desperately venomous but make you feel a bit ill, so his first thoughts were "I must get him some proper trousers." I don't know what trousers I wore prior to that, but anyway, and "boots, proper boots, farm boots," he said.'

Orwell's domestic diaries from this time are full of notes about planting vegetables, observations about the plant and animal life he saw and the weather. 'Very violent gale all last night and much rain,' he noted on 20 April. 'Could not do much out of doors.' And three days later: 'Dreadful weather till about 4pm. Violent wind, continuous rain, & very cold.'

But foul gardening weather is good writing weather and at the end of May the author wrote to Warburg: 'I have made a fairly good start on the book and think I must have written nearly a third of the first draft. I have got to as far as I hoped to by this time, because I have really been in most wretched health this year ever since about January (my chest as usual) and can't quite shake it off.' He hoped to have 'broken the back' of the first draft by October, while warning that his first drafts were 'always a ghastly mess'. Orwell's 'ghastly mess' perhaps echoed that of Gordon Comstock in *Keep the Aspidistra Flying*: 'A muddle of papers, perhaps two hundred sheets of sermon paper, grimy and dog-eared, and all written on and crossed out and written on again – a sort of sordid labyrinth of papers to which only Gordon possessed the key.'

While the inhabitants of Barnhill enjoyed a diet that included fish, lobster, rabbit, venison and fresh milk and eggs, many staples were in short supply in the island's only shop. A hint about the rigours of post-war rationing is to be found in Orwell's diary entry of 7 May: 'Began a new drum of paraffin today. Should last until end of July at least, *but NB to start agitating for a new drum some time in June.* [Orwell's emphasis]' Living without electric light made the writer terribly aware of his paraffin supplies. On the whole,

Barnhill: All but Drowned

Orwell was better off for fuel and food than he would have been in London, although 'the worst privation' was bread and petrol rationing. Fetching supplies from the shop in Craighouse once a week was a seldom avoidable extravagance paid in precious petrol, but sometimes Robin Fletcher drove up to Barnhill and Kinauchdrachd from Ardlussa with Orwell and the Darrochs' weekly rations, taking his daughter Fiona, who was about eight, and her little brother Alistair with him. Fiona didn't often see 'Mr Blair', as she called him: 'I think he'd be working in the house and Avril looked after us in the garden.'

Post-war shortages limited conviviality, as Orwell lamented to Sonia Brownell in one of the letters in which he incited her to visit him in vain: 'I have been able to arrange for alcohol so that one has just a little, a sort of rum ration, each day. Last year we had to be practically T.T.... . they can't get alcohol here at all easily. The next island, Islay, distils whisky, but it all goes to America.'[2]

Biographer Jeffrey Meyers describes Jura as 'one of the most unappealing and inaccessible places in the British isles'. Inaccessible, perhaps, but unappealing? It is, in fact, a beautiful and hospitable place attracting devoted visitors. But there is no doubt that Barnhill in the post-war years wasn't an easy place to live. Meyers believes that this was the attraction for Orwell: 'In many ways Orwell's austere and dour, Spartan and ascetic character as well as his tall, thin gangly figure were more Scottish than English. His compulsion to live an arduous and exhausting existence on the wet bog and windy moorland of Jura, in the country of Calvinism and oatcakes that he professed to dislike, was typically perverse – even suicidal.'[3]

Much has been made about the wisdom of a man with poor health moving to bracing Jura, and many scholarly eyebrows raised. 'A mad and suicidal sojourn', 'a suicidal residence', declared Jeffrey Meyers. 'A difficult and exhausting life ... in the worst possible climate,' opined Edward M. Thomas. 'It was a very bad idea. It killed him in the end,' Sonia Orwell told the BBC. 'Rash indeed for him to remain on the damp autumn and winter climate of the isles,' said George Woodcock, and Tosco Fyvel could never understand why Orwell couldn't have found a tranquil writer's haven somewhere in southern England with medical facilities close by.

In fact, the climate of this Inner Hebridean Island was far kinder to Orwell's ravaged lungs than smog-smothered London, and Barnhill farmhouse was a far more substantial building than the writer's damp and draught bedevilled tin-roofed cottage in Wallington. Although rainy and windy, Jura sits amid the warming Gulf Stream and decorative palm trees are not uncommon around the main settlement of Craighouse. Once he got his garden sorted, his lines baited, his crab and lobster creels out and his rifle in his hands, Orwell's diet was better too. On the downside, Barnhill was then seven miles from the nearest telephone. While the island did have a doctor, treatment for serious ills lay a twelve-hour journey by car, ferry and train to a Glasgow hospital. Even today ferries are cancelled because of storms. But in many ways the islanders of Jura lived, and still live, privileged lives in a beautiful, healthy and invigorating environment. As writer Alex Massie says in his introduction to a 2021 'Jura edition' of *Nineteen Eighty-Four*: 'If it was folly for him to live at Barnhill, it was folly for them to live in such an isolated place too.'

In mid-May Orwell was confined to bed for three days. 'Very sick until this morning,' he wrote in his diary on the twelfth. 'Got up for some hours this afternoon. Still shaky.' As soon as he was better, he went back to his smallholder ways, adding peat-cutting to his country skills. 'Cut 200 blocks, which takes 2 people 2 hours, including stripping off the turf before hand … we hope to cut not less than 1000 blocks in all.'

Barnhill: All but Drowned

Orwell now gave up the lease of his Wallington cottage that he had shared with Eileen, although he kept on the Canonbury Square flat as his occasional London lodging. Avril recalled that the summer of 1947 was wonderful, with her brother in good health and the house often full of visitors. 'R.R. crossing from Tarbert today, saw a large shark in the straight,' Orwell wrote in his diary. His old friend Richard Rees, who as the editor of the modernist literary journal *The Adelphi* had published some of Orwell's early work, arrived in early July for a painting holiday. Orwell had tempted him in a letter: 'You might find it rather paintable here. The colours on the sea are incredible but they change all the time. You could do some studies of real Highland cattle. They're all over the place, just like in Landseer's pictures.'

Rees found Orwell, Avril and Richard happy, but thought Barnhill was a good place for a strong man in perfect health to have a semi-camping holiday: 'I fear that the near impossibility of making a tolerably comfortable life there was a positive inducement to Orwell to settle in the remotest corner of the island of Jura.' Nevertheless, Rees put up with the discomfort and stayed for six weeks. He wrote that Orwell radiated an atmosphere of cosiness and told of how, arriving on one occasion at Barnhill at midnight, having left a truck of supplies bogged down in the rain on the track, he found Orwell 'had come down from his sick room, stoked up the kitchen fire and made preparations for supper, not merely with efficiency but with a comforting, hospitable, Dickensian glow.'[4]

Rees remembered: 'During his increasingly rare spells of good health he was certainly happy – working in the garden, fishing for mackerel from a boat, being bullied by his adopted son. He felt that he was at last putting down roots. But in reality, it was obvious that he had chosen a too rocky soil.'[5]

It was through Rees that young ex-soldier Bill Dunn was recruited that November to farm Barnhill's sixteen acres. Bill

Dunn had lost a leg below the knee to an anti-personnel mine in Sicily on 14 May 1944, which happened to be the day Orwell's son Richard was born. There is a strange synchronicity about this, as it was Bill's injury which led him to Jura and eventually the enormous role he would play in Richard's life. He recalled:

I went to Glasgow University during that awful winter of 1946 and did a term there studying for a B.Sc., in Agriculture. But I couldn't stick it, so I put an advert in the *Oban Times* saying I was available to anyone interested and I wanted to do some farming. I had no money at all. I got a reply from Robin Fletcher at Ardlussa, Jura and he invited me to stay for a couple of days and have a look over the place. Well, I liked it, and I liked Fletcher, so I decided to return, and I spent the summer of 1947 working for Fletcher's estate, not being paid but getting fed. It was a sort of reconnaissance, you might say.[6]

Dunn was lodging with Donald and Katie Darroch at Kinauchdrachd by the time Orwell and Avril returned, and met them when he visited Barnhill to collect some grass seed stored in an outbuilding there. His impression was that Orwell was unwell, but at first put that down to Orwell being wounded in the Spanish Civil War. The two men got on well enough while never becoming close friends, although Bill and Avril hit it off and used to go fishing together. 'I was just a friend of the family,' he recalled.

Although disabled, Bill Dunn impressed Richard Rees to the extent that Rees offered him £1,000 to farm Barnhill, with himself as the sleeping partner. Rees, a radical but wealthy intellectual, perhaps had a nostalgia for at least the idea of the simple life. And, as Orwell was keen to see Barnhill farmed, Rees may have thought he was doing his friend a favour by further enticing Dunn to stay on Jura. Dunn jumped at the offer of land to farm for himself and moved into Barnhill with Orwell and Avril. ''I don't know what he thought of me moving in with him and Avril. There was no suggestion of disapproval. In fact it was with his approval that I went there. It seemed the obvious thing to do. Orwell was the tenant at Barnhill. But I leased land from the Fletchers.'

Living in Barnhill, Dunn could hear the writer at work, typing, in his big upstairs bedroom with its view of the sea. He knew nothing of what Orwell was working on but would sometimes take him a cup of tea. The window would be closed and the air thick with the smoke of the 'awful, thick black tobacco' Orwell constantly smoked and the fumes of the paraffin stove. 'It must have been terribly bad for him,' Dunn thought. Although Orwell occasionally fished, it would make him tired and most days he stayed in his room and wrote all day. Dunn recalled: 'But always in the evening – about five, at teatime – he would chat for a bit and maybe discuss the news on the wireless, and then he'd say, "Gosh, I should go and do some work." And that would be the last time we'd see him that day. Ricky would only really see him during the day.'

Another ex-soldier to arrive in north Jura was Tony Rozga, one of many thousands of Polish ex-servicemen who made their lives in Scotland after their homeland was annexed by the Soviet Union in a deal hatched by the victorious Allied powers at Yalta in Crimea. Tony had been involved in training Commandos at Inveraray, and the Scots girl who became his wife was a cook in the NAAFI there. Soon married and demobbed, Tony started looking for work: 'There was a job advertised, and I applied and was interviewed by Robin Fletcher. I came from a farming community and loved to work on the land, and after the war I wanted a house and peace and quiet. I loved the place when I saw it. The salary was five pounds a week and free house and two cows for milking. I got the job after two Scots boys refused it.'[7]

Although married, Tony Rozga initially arrived alone, moving into Kinauchdrachd once the Darrochs had move to the centre of Jura to work for the Astors' estate, and Orwell and Avril sometimes invited him to tea. Rozga claimed that his English was poor in those early days but that he liked to hear Orwell talk. He was also given a copy of *Animal Farm*, and doubtless Orwell thought it would be appreciated by a man whose country – the German invasion of which had brought Britain into the war – had been betrayed to Stalin's dictatorship. 'He gave it to me as a present,' Rozga said. 'I didn't ask him why he came to Jura, but the impression I got was that he came for much the same reason as I did: hiding from people, fed up with the war, fed up with people. Hiding oneself in a corner and enjoying life …'

Once, when soaked and frozen after retrieving a duck he had shot from the sea, Rozga was given a double black rum by Orwell, who would also give him shag tobacco, refusing payment, when Rozga ran out of cigarettes. Orwell customarily greeted Rozga with a wave, and the Pole was convinced that Orwell was happy at Barnhill, despite being ill. Tony Rozga was soon joined by his wife Jeannie, who also had fond memories of Orwell, and the couple would visit the writer in Barnhill perhaps twice a week. Jeannie's son Blair recalls: 'They became friends, and mum and Avril had a lot in common. They were both townies, stuck really in the middle of nowhere, virtually the back of beyond, so you can understand why they would become friends. They were friends and neighbours even though they were living a mile apart.'[8]

Jean and Tony Rozga knew Orwell had written the best-selling *Animal Farm*, but Jeannie recalled: 'We didn't think of him as a "famous person." He didn't come across that way. To me George Orwell was a tall, quiet, gentle man. I was quite surprised when I read *Nineteen Eighty-Four*. I couldn't believe it; he didn't seem that sort of person. I thought, "Fancy him writing that sort of book." I would have imagined something gentler.'

Jeannie and Tony Rozga named one of their sons Blair, the surname Orwell went by on Jura. Blair Rozga reflects: 'They never said to me that I was named after Eric Blair, but Blair's not a family name. They just liked the name Blair and I think it's a very good chance I was named after him.' Blair Rozga is a successful farmer on the neighbouring island of Islay, and there are still Rozga decedents on Jura.[9]

Knowing Tony Rozga put a human face on a growing canker in Scotland that disturbed Orwell – the rise of anti-Polish feeling against ex-servicemen unable or afraid to return to their native country now under Stalinist rule. While overnighting in a Glasgow hotel, Orwell eavesdropped on the conversation of two small-business owners who deplored the presence of Poles in Scotland. Their gripe was that Poles were buying up all the flats and houses ('where they get the money from is a mystery'), invading the medical profession, were 'very degraded in their morals' and that there were already too many people in Britain. Writing in *Tribune*, Orwell noted: 'It is the contemporary equivalent of antisemitism.' He reasoned that by 1947 the kind of people who, pre-revelations of the holocaust, had been anti-Semitic now found that stance discreditable but sought their scapegoats elsewhere. Polish refugees were now the scapegoats of choice. What most depressed Orwell was that the two men repeatedly used the phrase 'let them go back to their own country':

If I had said to these two business-men, 'Most of these people have no country to go back to.' They would have gaped. Not one of the relevant facts would have been known to them. They would never have heard of the various things that have happened to Poland since 1939, any more than they would have known that the over-population of Britain is a fallacy or that local unemployment can co-exist with a general shortage of labour. I think it is a mistake to give such people the excuse of ignorance. You can't actually change their feelings, but you can make them understand what they are saying when they demand that homeless refugees shall be driven from our shores, and the knowledge may make them a little less actively malignant.[10]

Orwell later learned that out of twenty-six Poles repatriated to Poland from Scotland in January 1947, twenty-three had been arrested and charged with spying by Stalin's puppet regime.[11]

*

Orwell welcomed guests at Barnhill but would keep his distance from them if busy or unwell. Jeannie Rozga remembers:

> Eric had this big marquee in the garden where he used to sleep sometimes. We went over maybe twice a week, and he would hear us and come in, and if he'd had a bad day we wouldn't see him, but if he'd had a good day he'd come and join in. He liked company. He had a huge number of friends, and they were real friends, believe you me, to come all that way to see him, even in the middle of winter. And I don't think there was a week went past without someone coming up and staying. And they would stay for ages.

A letter of Avril's to her brother-in-law Humphrey Dakin reveals that at one time the Barnhill household had swollen to eleven, overflowing into a tent. 'Mostly men, so dead sea fruit[12] as far as any help to me went.'

In the summer of 1947 Eileen's sister-in-law Gwen O'Shaughnessy arrived with her daughters on Jura for a week, as did Jane and Lucy Dakin, the daughters of his late sister Marjorie, and their brother Henry, a second lieutenant on leave from the army. Jane Dakin, recently released from war work in the Women's' Land Army, recalled her Barnhill days with affection: 'Barnhill was a lovely house, with a lovely kitchen, a proper farm kitchen with an old-fashioned range. It was cosy because Avril was a very relaxed sort of person, really, and had the knack of making the place seem cosy, even though she wasn't a neat and tidy person. But she created a welcoming atmosphere.'[13]

After breakfast Jane's Uncle Eric would go to his room and write until lunch, the main meal of the day. Mealtimes were fun with plenty of chat and although Orwell didn't 'hold forth' he liked having lots of chat going on and was a good listener. He would often make funny comments and then laugh at his own jokes. She noticed that her uncle loved 'steamed puds' and liked the way he made appreciative noises when he ate them. Aunt Avril – or 'Av' – was the more talkative of the Blair siblings. 'A chatty individual,' said her nephew Henry. 'She talked our kind of language.' Jane remembered that evenings with Orwell could be quite convivial: 'He never worried about furniture or elegant clothes or cars, etc., but he did like food, and after fishing for mackerel or saithe in the evening, or walking to get milk in a Scotch mist, there were cries of "brandy and milk, brandy and milk", and people sat around the kitchen talking and drinking.'

To entertain Richard and the three young Dakins, Orwell arranged an expedition to Glengarrisdale Bay on the uninhabited west side of the island where there was a fine beach and an old shepherd's cottage they could camp in. 'No beds, but otherwise quite comfortable,' he wrote. 'There are beautiful white beaches round that side, and if you do about an hour's climb into the hills you come to lochs which are full of trout but never fished because unget-atable.' Orwell took Ricky, Henry and Lucy round in his twelve-foot dinghy while Jane and Avril walked by the rough path that crossed the island. Lucy Dakin distinctly remembers Bill Dunn warning: 'Well, are you sure about the tides? Very dangerous, Corryvreckan, very dangerous.' The *Swiss Family Robinson* existence at Glengarrisdale Bay lasted a couple of days while Orwell and Henry fished for trout in a lochan and Avril cooked them with bacon. Lucy was shocked when Jane and her aunt Av bathed in the nude – and Jane and Av were even more shocked when a Navy vessel hove into view and they had to scuttle for cover. When it was time to return to Barnhill, Orwell loaded the dinghy with the camping gear and – after a great discussion about tides – he, Ricky, Henry and Lucy set off in the boat while the rest of the party walked back. Jane remembered: 'The boat looked so full and unsafe that Av and I elected to walk home.'[14]

Decades later, Richard Blair, who became a skilful yachtsman, recalled his father's failings as a mariner: 'It was when we were coming back, into Corryvreckan, that my father misread the tide-time, which was probably not difficult since he had made it up himself, so it wasn't an official tide-table, it was one that he had worked out, and we arrived at Corryvreckan and the tide was still running on the flood and we got ourselves into all sort of trouble.'[15]

Before relating the story of the incident which nearly took four lives and cost the world a literary masterpiece, it is worth considering other accounts of the notorious Corryvreckan. Its very name gives a fair description of this troubled and challenging seaway, coming from the Gaelic Coire Bhreacain, meaning 'cauldron of the speckled seas' or 'cauldron of the plaid'. A fierce tidal race, a standing wave and whirlpools make it a challenge even for experienced seamen in sturdy craft. The Clyde Cruising Club's *Sailing Directions* states: 'The warnings which invariably accompany descriptions of this notorious gulf should be carefully heeded ...' It then goes on to describe the Corryvreckan's 'ferocious nature under certain conditions of wind and tide'. In 1549 the Scottish clergyman Dean Monro wrote: 'Betwixt thir two Ilis their runs aye stream above the power of all sailing and rowing with infinite dangeris callit Arey brekan.' Another classic description of the Corryvreckan was given by the Scottish traveller Martin Martin:

Between the north end of Jura and the Isle of Scarba, lies the famous and dangerous gulf, called Cry Vrekan, about a Mile in breadth; it yields an impetuous Current, not to be matched anywhere about the Isle of Britain. The sea begins to boil and ferment with the Tide at Flood, and resembles the boiling of a Pot; and then increases gradually, until it appears in many Whirlpools, which form themselves in sort of Pyramids, and immediately after a spout up as high as the mast of a little Vessel, and at the same time make a loud report.[16]

Michael Powell, the director of the classic 1945 film *I Know Where I'm Going!*, which was shot mostly on Mull, took a motorboat into the Corryvreckan to film shots with his faithful 35mm Eyemo movie camera. Powell described how his boat pitched and tossed and sometimes whirled right round in the boiling sea, and that he had to tie himself to the mast to operate his camera: 'My particular triumph was to snatch with the camera one of these mysterious boils which comes roaring up from unknown depths … by now, Corryvreckin would be roaring, and if the wind was against the tide, the minor races would be yelling and screaming and you could hear the din twenty miles out at sea.'[17]

As Orwell's dinghy chugged towards the Corryvreckan Lucy Dakin recalled that the waves began to get bigger and that the little outboard engine was labouring. Her brother remarked: 'I think we must be getting nearer to the whirlpool.' Henry remembered:

Round the edges of the whirlpool were dozens of smaller whirl-pools. We weren't in the main surge. We were flung this way and that. Eric was at the tiller. There was a cracking noise, and the engine came straight off its mountings and disappeared intro the sea. And Eric said, 'I think you'd better get the oars out, Henry.' And he patted his chest and sort of said, 'I can't help you, Hen, of course.' And so the oars were fished out of this wildly swaying and swinging boat. Everybody was fairly calm. The kids were thinking it was a bit of an adventure. I think Eric and I thought it was a little more than that.[18]

The fit young soldier pulled manfully on the oars, but the boat made little headway through the whirlpool, although he did manage to steady it somewhat. Three-year-old Ricky was enjoy-ing himself, chanting: 'Up-down, splish-splosh.' A seal popped its head up to stare at the boat and Orwell remarked calmly about how inquisitive seals were. Orwell was masking his deep concern but Lucy, beginning to get frightened, did not find the remark useful or comforting. Her uncle later confided in his diary: 'Ran into the whirlpool and were all nearly drowned. Engine sucked off by the sea and went to the bottom.'[19]

Henry reckoned that the whirlpool was subsiding, not rising, and that his uncle had only miscalculated the tides by half an hour. Pulling strenuously at the oars, he managed to edge the over-laden craft towards the islet of Eilean Mor, about half a mile off Jura. Even when they got under its lea, Henry feared that the Atlantic rollers were still likely to swamp the boat and he took his army boots off in case they had to swim for it. Eventually, they found themselves in smoother water about 100 yards from the island. As the dinghy got close to the rocky coastline, Henry leapt from the boat onto a ledge and began pulling it ashore with its mooring rope. As he did so, the swell caused the dinghy to turn turtle, throwing the others into the water. Henry saw Lucy appear from under it … then his Uncle Eric … but there was no sign of Ricky who was trapped under the boat.

Richard Blair recalled: 'I'm sitting on my father's knee and we ended up underneath the boat.' Groping under the upturned dinghy, Orwell caught his son's leg and dragged him out. Henry remembered: 'Eric had grabbed him as the boat turned and pulled him out from under the boat. He had to swim from the end of the boat to the side of the island, still hanging on to Ricky. He seemed to keep his normal "Uncle Eric" face the whole time, no panic from him or anyone.' Henry managed to haul all three of the family ashore, although all the equipment on the boat was lost.

'The whole thing was OK,' Richard recalled, 'but of course it could have turned very nasty. My father could have banged his head. Who knows what could have happened? These sort of accidents at sea could turn into a tragedy in the twinkling of an eye.' Richard's line is chillingly similar to Finlay Currie's as the wise old ferryman Ruairidh Mhór in Michael Powell's *I Know Where I'm Going!*: 'In less than a second, you could get from this world into the next.' Out of earshot of Lucy and Ricky, Orwell admitted to Henry that he thought they had had it. 'I agreed,' testified Henry years later. 'I thought we were lucky to get out of it. Really.'

After they had been on the island for half an hour or so, a small lobster boat appeared. Orwell wrote that it had been attracted by a signal fire they had lit with his remarkably resilient cigarette lighter. Henry remembered: 'It picked us up with some difficulty because of the swell and had to throw a rope across and we clambered along the rope one by one, Eric taking Ricky on his back.' The fisherman was Donald Mackay, from Toberonochy on the island of Luing, one of the slate quarrying islands to the north of Jura in the Firth of Lorn. Fortunately for Orwell and his fellow castaways, Mackay had, like many Hebrideans then and since, several jobs. He fished for crabs and lobsters, delivered mail and provisions to the island of Shuna, and took tourists in his boat on sight-seeing tours. It was on such tour that he discovered Orwell's party. 'They took us off,' recalled Lucy. 'They were going to offer to take us round to Barnhill. I'd lost one shoe in all this, and scraped my ankle, and Henry hadn't got any shoes, but Eric, who had got both *his* shoes, said, "Oh no, it's all right, we'll walk back." I remember being furious.' It was a four- or five-mile hike to Barnhill and Orwell strode off with Ricky on his back while Lucy and Henry limped behind. Lucy remembered that Jane and Avril were hay-making when the party returned. 'They looked up and said, "I thought you were coming back by boat." And Eric said, "Oh, we lost the boat," without any mention of the drama that had taken place, with a calm acceptance of things that was typical of Uncle Eric. He was sweet and kind, but in another world.' Bill Dunn had been among the haymakers and remembered Orwell's bedraggled arrival: 'He was furious that no one had sent a rescue party. Avril got her own back saying, "Well you told us you never bothered if people came late." He said, "That's right, that's quite right …"'

Henry recalled that such was the offhand way Orwell talked about the loss of the boat that Jane and Av took some convincing that they really had been wrecked in the Corryvreckan. Orwell, typically, made little of the near fatal adventure. In a letter to George Woodcock, he describes the days spent in the shepherd's hut by the beautiful beaches on the west coast of Jura – but failed to mention the Corryvreckan incident at all. In a letter to Anthony Powell, Orwell confessed to 'being all but drowned' in the shipwreck and 'being literally wrecked on a desert island where we might have been stranded for a day or two … Richard loved every moment of it except when he was actually in the water.' And to Celia Kirwan, Orwell admitted: 'The awful thing was having Richard with us.'

Later, while in Hairmyres Hospital, Orwell heard from Avril that Richard had suddenly become afraid of boats. He wrote to a friend: 'Previously he wasn't at all frightened in a boat, indeed not enough so, & liked to hang over the side in the most dangerous way. When we were nearly drowned in the Corrievrechan, he seemed to take the whole experience in his stride, but I think his present fear may be a delayed reaction to that.'[20] Orwell dismissed the damage the shipwreck had done to himself. In later years Richard recalled: 'It certainly didn't do my father's health much good, because his lungs flared up again and he was not at all well later on.'

Avril recalled: 'At the end of the summer 1947, it became obvious that my brother was ill, and we thought he'd better consult a doctor.'[21] Despite his ill-health, Orwell decided to over-winter on Jura. He told a friend: 'I can work here with fewer interruptions, and I think we shall be less cold here. The climate, though wet, is not quite so cold as in England, and it is much easier to get fuel.' Peat and wood, some of it driftwood, helped spin out the precious coal, which was rationed until 1958.

In a 1965 BBC TV interview, Malcolm Muggeridge asked Avril if her brother thought he was writing against time. 'I don't think so because I don't think he was the sort of person who thought he was going to die – not immediately anyway,' she replied. 'He knew he was ill but I don't think he ever entertained what is commonly called the death wish.'

On 7 November 1947, Orwell completed the first draft of *Nineteen-Eighty-Four*, but his health was failing and he had not seen a doctor for a year. Orwell was now bedridden, unable to work and fretting about the state of his novel. He only considered his rough draft the halfway mark to completion. He wrote to Anthony Powell:

I'm still on my back, but I think really getting better after many relapses. I'd probably be all right by this time if I could have got to my usual chest specialists, but I dare not make the journey to the mainland while I have a temperature. It's really a foul journey in winter even if one flies part of the way. However I've now arranged for a man to come from Glasgow & give me the once-over ...[22]

In early December the chest specialist from Glasgow travelled to the Fletchers' home at Ardlussa to examine Orwell and diagnosed him as having TB with complications. The doctor warned him against the bumpy road back to Barnhill and, despite having young children who might be infected, Margaret Fletcher was prepared to take necessary hygienic precautions and let him stay at Ardlussa. Her daughter Fiona recalled: 'She was one of these people who was very good and went out of her way to be kind.' Orwell refused Margaret Fletcher's bold and generous offer, and Richard Rees drove Orwell's vehicle down from Barnhill to take him back there. Before he left Ardlussa, Margaret's husband Robin spent some time talking to him – he was convinced that Orwell knew he was gravely ill and racing against time to finish his book.[23]

Back at Barnhill Orwell was haunted by the fear of passing on TB to Ricky, while longing to spend enough time with him to bond closely as father and son. Orwell's father had been absent for most of his young life, and he was determined to have a closer and more loving relationship with his own son. Richard remembers his father being confined to bed for days at a time, but recalled: 'When he played with me, he treated me as if he were quite fit and healthy. I was always happy when he'd appear to play or just to talk. I think he bore his illness with great fortitude.' During Orwell's all too short time with Richard he did manage to create a bond that endured after his death. 'I feel that I was his son, part of him,' Richard Blair told CBC in 1983. 'He was my father – there was no question about it, although I'd been adopted by him. He was my father.'

Writing to a friend, Orwell apologised for his briefness, citing his illness and the fact that he'd been bedridden for six weeks, had been feeling unwell before that, and was being sent to a sanatorium for treatment. 'It's an awful bore,' he complained, 'however perhaps it's all for the best if they can cure me. I don't think living on Jura has had a bad effect on my health – in any case the sanatorium I'm going to is near Glasgow, which is the same climate. Actually we've had marvellous weather this year & very dry.'[24]

CHAPTER 10

That Bloody Book

'It isn't a book I would gamble on for a big sale.'

—George Orwell, letter to Fred Warburg

Five days before Christmas 1947, Orwell entered Hairmyres Hospital at East Kilbride, less than twenty miles from Glasgow. He wrote to his sister-in-law Gwen O'Shaughnessy telling her that he believed his family had had quite a good Christmas, but that he was glad to have got away before then 'so as not to be a death's head'. A private man, he found the hospital Christmas celebrations 'harrowing, with the "parties" they have – all the beds dragged into one ward, & then a concert & a Christmas tree.' On New Year's Eve he wrote to Tosco Fyvel:

> I've only been in this hospital abt. 10 days, but I've been deadly sick for abt 2-3 months & not very well the whole year. Of course I've had this disease before, but not so seriously. I was very well last year, & I think this show really started in that beastly cold of last winter. I was conscious early this year of being seriously ill and thought I'd probably got T.B., but like a fool I decided not to go to a doctors as I knew I'd be stuck in bed and I wanted to get on with the book I was writing ... However, they seem pretty confident they can patch me up, so I might be able to get back to some serious work some time in 1948.

Orwell told Fyvel of the measures he and Avril were taking to avoid Richard contracting TB – keeping him at arm's length as best he could, boiling his milk and getting a TB-tested cow – but noted with pleasure that his son looked fit and robust.

'He is developing into a regular tough and loves working on the farm & messing abt with machinery.' Orwell – with the threat of nuclear war in mind – ends the letter on a depressing note: 'This stupid war is coming off in about 10 to 20 years, and this country will be blown off the map whatever else happens. The only hope is to have a home with a few animals in some place not worth a bomb.'[1]

In a memoir, Fyvel speculated that Orwell may really have believed that by moving to Jura he was protecting himself and his young son from the atomic threat. Earlier that year Orwell had written an essay for an American magazine that expressed in journalism much of the background to the novel he was writing. The fear of mutually assured destruction might prevent nuclear war – but would lead to worldwide totalitarianism.

> It would mean the division of the world among two or three vast super-states, unable to conquer each other and unable to be over-thrown by any internal rebellion. In all probability their structure would be hierarchic, with a semi-divine cast at the top and outright slavery at the bottom, and the crushing out of liberty would exceed anything that the world has yet seen. Within each state the necessary psychological atmosphere would be kept up by complete severance from the outer world, and by a continuous phony war against rival states.[2]

Had Orwell used the words 'Inner Party', 'proles' 'Thought Police' and 'Two Minutes Hate' in that paragraph, he might have being writing the blurb for *Nineteen Eighty-Four*. Less than two years earlier, Orwell had coined the name for the fearful stasis that states armed with nuclear weapons found themselves in – Cold War.[3] The phrase would come to define an era and become another potent 'Orwellian' expression to enter the English language.

*

Consultant Dr Bruce Dick, the specialist in charge of the Thoracic Unit at Hairmyres, revealed that Orwell's TB was 'chronic'. Dick was an 'offensively jolly, heavy drinking character' who was 'given to slapping his patients on the back and exhorting them in a hearty manner'.[4] In other words, the extrovert yin to Orwell's introvert yang. David Astor reported that Orwell believed that Dick had served with Franco's forces during the war in Spain and that the author of *Homage to Catalonia* was amused by the thought that the dedicated specialist now trying to save his life had been a fascist who would have once been glad to see him killed. Dr James Williamson, Dick's junior doctor, later described that story as 'bunkum'.

Williamson, appointed to Hairmyres in February 1948, saw Orwell almost every day for the rest of the writer's seven-month stay. He remembered Orwell having a private room in Ward 3 that was crammed with books.[5] Although Orwell felt his mind clear, his curiosity undimmed, and could read, he found serious writing impossible and *Nineteen Eighty-Four* lay neglected. 'This is a very nice hospital and everyone is most kind to me, and I have a room to myself,' he wrote to a friend. 'I'm starting to attempt a very little work ... an occasional book review, after doing nothing for three months.'[6]

Williamson told the BBC *Arena* team:

I remember quite clearly. He had quite extensive disease in both lungs but it was principally his left lung that was affected. It was a very chronic fibrotic disease, not like the classic galloping consumption of the 19th century which the Brontës suffered from, and he was never terribly ill in the sense that he wasn't toxic or fevered or didn't waste away to any great extent, but he must have felt pretty sub-standard most of the time. And of course he had a chronic cough, not helped by the fact that he smoked almost incessantly.[7]

And Williamson told CBC: 'He was never very ill with severe wasting and drenching night sweats ... but he'd probably forgotten, almost, what it was to feel completely well. It was what we call fibrotic tuberculosis. His lung would have been tough, like leather. With chronic fibrotic TB you could live for quite a long while, although at a lower level of health and fitness and comfort, as he did. He lived for many years with TB.'[8]

The treatment Orwell underwent was brutal. His worst affected lung, the left, was regularly pierced, collapsed and re-inflated with oxygen. 'But he never complained,' remembered Williamson, 'in fact we all noticed how much self-control he had. There was never a gasp, or any kind of noise from him when we did this.' David Astor, one of Orwell's closest and most loyal friends, travelled from London to visit him several times:

He'd become much thinner, but he was always a person who had a 'presence,' whether he was dying or not, and you couldn't help treating him as himself. He didn't ask for pity. The really awful part of the treatment was that they put a sort of rod down this throat, slithered it down, to look at his lungs. In those days it was the only way they could find out. It was a hideously painful thing, and very frightening. He spoke of this with a fair amount of horror. I felt in *Nineteen Eighty-Four* the torture scenes could have derived from the sensations of this experience.[9]

The treatment brought Orwell relief but did not cure him. Meanwhile news of a new wonder drug, developed in the USA, had reached Bruce Dick. The first patient treated with experimental antibiotic Streptomycin had died, the second had recovered although had gone blind as a side effect, but the third person, treated in March 1946, had made a rapid and full recovery.[10]

In February 1948 Orwell wrote to his publisher Fred Warburg saying that had it not been for is ill-health he might have finished the book by May. As it stood, he explained, it was 'just a ghastly mess', but he was convinced that the idea was good and couldn't possibly abandon it. Yet, his ill-health preyed on his mind, and he told Warburg: 'If anything should happen to me I've instructed Richard Rees, my literary executor, to destroy the MS [manuscript] without showing it to anybody, but it's unlikely that anything like that would happen. This disease isn't dangerous at my age, and they say the cure is going on quite well, though slowly … We are now sending for some new American drug called streptomycin which they say will speed up the cure.'

Wealthy and influential, David Astor managed to secure and import enough of the 'wonder drug' to treat Orwell. And, for a while, it worked. 'I am getting a lot better,' the patient told Julian Symons. 'I have been having the streptomycin for abt a month, & evidently it is doing its stuff. I haven't gained much weight, but I am much better in every other way, & longing to get up, which of course they won't let me do for ages yet.'

Streptomycin's first British guineapig did not respond well. Orwell's lungs and breathing improved and he put on weight during his six months in Hairmyres, but the side effects of the little-tested medication were serious and Orwell – in the words of Dr Williamson – suffered 'a fearful allergic reaction'. His throat became dry and inflamed, yet he had difficulty swallowing liquids to relieve it and he suffered from ulcers, rashes and hair loss. Later, doctors learned that if a patient was given a tiny dose, and that this was gradually increased to just the verge of an allergic reaction, he would become desensitized to the drug and be able to complete the treatment. But this was unknown in the early days. 'If it had been two or three years later, it would have been pretty easy to cure his TB,' said Williamson. 'But he might still have died from a haemorrhage because the haemorrhage was really a sort of indirect result of the TB.' David Astor lamented of the miracle cure: 'It came too late, by quite a long chalk too late.'[11]

Gradually, the patient began to improve, although summoning the energy and focus to write was difficult. Orwell confided to his diary: 'It is only when you attempt to write, even to write the simplest & stupidest newspaper article, that you realise what a deterioration has happened inside your skull ... Your mind turns away to any conceivable subject rather than the one you are trying to deal with ...'[12]

Orwell was pleased with the treatment he got at Hairmyres, and while resigned to never regaining full health, itched to get back to Jura.

> I am longing to get up to Jura at any rate for a few days, to see Richard & see how the farm work is going, but I shall have to be careful not to do too much. I'm afraid that even when completely cured I shall be not much good physically for the rest of my life – I never was strong or athletic, but I don't like an altogether sedentary life, & I shall have to readjust my habits so that I can get abt without making too much muscular effort, no more digging or chopping wood, for instance.[13]

In May he told a friend: 'I've started revising the novel, but I do only a very little, perhaps an hour's work each day. However at that rate I should get through several chapters before leaving hospital.'[14]

For a man who had dedicated the past twenty years of his life to writing, the period of creative inactivity – he was forbidden to use his typewriter – must have been deeply frustrating, but it was not his greatest concern. He confided to Julian Symons: 'What chiefly worries me is Richard, whom I haven't seen for four or five months.'[15] Avril sent photographs and noted that Richard 'is evidently growing enormous'.

Orwell had come to realise that he had been close to death and that he was lucky to be alive for Richard, and to compete his novel:

> The book I am at work on was to be finished at the beginning of this year – now it can't be finished before the end of the year, which means not coming out till the end of 1949. However it's something to be capable of working again. Last year before they brought me here I really felt as though I were finished. Thank Heaven Richard looks as if he is going to have good health.[16]

On 25 June 1948 Orwell celebrated his forty-fifth birthday in Hairmyres. He complained to Anthony Powell in a letter about his growing number of false teeth and greying hair but reported that he was now up and about for three hours a day, often playing croquet which, after six months on his back, he found quite tough. He'd also met a fellow journalist who was a patient in the ward below his – the editor of *The Hotspur*. The D.C. Thomson story paper for boys had been discussed in Orwell's 1940 essay *Boys' Weeklies*, and Orwell was doubtless fascinated how such a magazine was put together, although he found the man rather dull. *The Hotspur* editor told him that his writers regularly turned in 40,000 words a week and one had done 70,000 but his work was 'rather stereotyped'.

Orwell wrote that he was 'tinkering' with his novel and had hopes of completing it by the end of the year. He was also eagerly anticipating a visit from Richard, whom he hadn't seen since Christmas and worried that the child would hardly know him. In early July Avril made the arduous journey from Jura to East Kilbride so that Richard could visit his father at Hairmyres

– strictly out of doors – and thought that the visits did her brother an enormous amount of good. Orwell wrote of Richard to a friend: 'He is tremendously well and almost frighteningly energetic. His talking still seems backwards, but in other ways I should say he was forward. Farm life seems to suit him, though I am pretty sure he is one for machines rather than animals.' Orwell was determined not to push Richard unwillingly along a book-learning path, telling David Astor: 'I remember the miseries I went through because of the then-prevalent idea that you were half-witted if you couldn't read before you were six.'[17]

A release date from Hairmyres was set for 25 July,[18] and Orwell told Julian Symons that he was looking forward to getting 'home' – which was Jura, much to Avril's annoyance. She recalled: 'When he came out, he looked comparatively fit, but he would insist on coming back to Barnhill which he loved. I suppose he wanted to live there in order to go on with his writing. If he'd gone into a convalescent home then, he probably would have been cured, but as it was he came back and insisted on living a quite ordinary life. It really was extremely stupid.'[19]

Orwell returned to Barnhill under strict orders to do no physical work, although Bill Dunn recalled that Avril would sometimes have to wrest a barrow or rake from his hands to stop him. 'Sometimes one doesn't have an awful lot of authority over one's own family, and he never really was one much to listen to other people,' said Avril. Bill Dunn recalled to CBC that once back in Barnhill Orwell began work on the second draft of his book. 'He worked at it all the time. And his health began going down. I think he felt pretty ill.'

Dr James Williamson believed that when Orwell returned to Barnhill he wasn't coughing a lot and would not have been terribly infectious, although still a potential danger to others, particularly to his young son. Desperate to see and spend time with Ricky, Orwell was able to play with the child but had to discourage the close contact he must have craved, although Richard has made the point that the Blairs were a product of their time and class and were not 'a huggy-kissy sort of family'.

Orwell was, however, aware that the relationship between his forty-one-year-old sister and the decade younger Bill Dunn had become closer than that that of a landlady and her lodger or even a family friend. Biographer Bernard Crick suggests that Orwell 'soon mastered his lower-upper-middle class prejudice and saw the bright side of it, growing to accept the situation'.

In October Orwell visited Hairmyres to be examined. He wrote to David Astor:

> Dr. Dick seems to be quite pleased with the results of his exam-
> ination, but the journey upset me. Any kind of journey seems
> to do this. He told me to go on as at present, i.e. spending half
> the day in bed, which I quite gladly do as I simply can't manage
> any kind of exertion. To walk a mile or pick up anything in the
> least heavy, or above all to get cold, promptly upsets me. Even
> if I go out in the evening to fetch the cows in it gives me a tem-
> perature. On the other hand, so long as I live a senile sort of life
> I feel all right, and I seem to be able to work much as usual. I
> have got so used to writing in bed that I think I prefer it, though
> of course it's awkward to type there. I am just struggling with
> the last pages of this bloody book which is supposed be done
> by early December, and will be if I don't get ill again. It would
> have been done by the spring if it had not been for this illness.[20]

Throughout this challenging time Orwell plugged on at his book, tapping away in his upstairs room at Barnhill. Other than telling people that his book would probably be called *The Last Man in Europe*, he was his usual secretive self about it. 'I can't show you the part-finished novel,' he told his close friend Julian

Symons. 'I never show them to anybody, because they are just a mess & don't have much relationship to the final draft. I always say a book doesn't exist until it is finished.' Richard Blair has said that his father dodged even his close friend Richard Rees's enquiries about the subject of his new novel by gnomically holding up four fingers and asking: 'How many fingers am I holding up?' When Rees replied: 'Four,' Orwell replied mischievously: 'Could be five!'

While Orwell had learned the skill of typing much of his journalism straight onto paper in a form that could be sent for typesetting, his novels were a very different matter. Like Beethoven, he scored out and scribbled on his first thoughts repeatedly. 'I always alter (my books) a good deal in rewriting,' he once told Cyril Connolly. And so, one of the most famous opening sentences in the history of English literature:

It was a bright cold day in April, and the clocks were striking thirteen.

… previously read:

It was a cold blowy day in early April, and a million radios were striking thirteen.

… and:

It was a cold blowy day in early April and innumerable clocks were striking thirteen.

The fascinating facsimile edition of *Nineteen Eighty-Four* allows scholars and fans to marvel at the painstaking effort spent on each line of the book and justifies Orwell's line from his essay *Why I Write*: 'Writing a book is a horrible, exhausting struggle, like a long bout of some painful illness.'[21]

He told his close friend and publisher Fred Warburg: 'I am not pleased with the book but I am not absolutely dissatisfied. I first thought of it in 1943. I think it is a good idea but the execution would have been better if I had not written it under the influence of TB. I haven't definitely fixed on the title but I am hesitating between *Nineteen Eighty-Four* and *The Last Man in Europe*.'[22]

Later that month, in a long letter to writer Julian Symons, Orwell revealed his fears for the future and how his love for his son magnified these fears.

Richard is blooming. He is still I think a little backward about talking, but lively enough in other ways and really almost helpful about the farm and garden. Something tells me he won't be one for book-learning and that his bent is for mechanics. I shan't try and influence him, but if he grew up with the ambition of being a farmer I should be pleased. Of course that may be the only job left after the atom bombs. If the show does start and is as bad as one fears, it would be fairly easy to be self-supporting on these islands provided one wasn't looted.[23]

Orwell added that he didn't expect a 'shooting war' for five or ten years but thought that once the Russians got atomic bombs it would be unavoidable.[24]

In November 1848 Orwell descended the stairs from his room, entered the kitchen and announced to Avril and Bill Dunn: 'Well, I've finished it.' Dunn recalled: 'We celebrated by opening the last bottle of wine we had in the place. And Avril said to him, "What's the title, what are you going to call it?" And he said, "I think *Nineteen Eighty-Four*." Orwell was characteristically downbeat about his efforts and convinced that his illness had prevented him from giving it his best. He wrote to Anthony Powell: 'It's awful to think that I've been mucking about with this book since June

1947, and it's a ghastly mess now, a good idea ruined, but of course I was seriously ill for 7 or 8 months of the time.'

In wretched health, having written a darkly dystopian novel and worrying about his young son and the possible destruction of millions of people in a nuclear war, Orwell could have no inkling that he had written one of the most important books in world literature. 'It isn't a book I would gamble on for a big sale,' he warned his publisher Fred Warburg, and told Julian Symons that he had 'ballsed it up, rather'.

Orwell's manuscript is fascinating – corrected throughout with overtyping, scorings out and corrections in pen – but it was not in a fit state to send to a publisher. Orwell turned to Warburg for help in getting a corrected manuscript typed, telling him: 'A skilled typist under my eye could do it easily enough.' In 1970 Warburg told Melvyn Bragg, for the BBC's *Omnibus*:

He wrote and asked me to find him a secretary to go up to Jura, where you had to cross two lots of sea, and then go on a mule for five miles, and the last five miles you walked.[25] So it was not a very attractive job for a London typist. And I tried quite a few, but they wouldn't go. Had one of them gone, he might have been able to finish *Nineteen Eighty-Four* without breaking his neck over it. But I couldn't find him one and he typed it all himself – very well – and it came in, as all his books did come in to us, in a virtual perfect condition, with hardly a comma wrong.

Orwell told Anthony Powell that he was 'on the grisly job' of typing out the novel himself, and doggedly tapped out up to 5,000 words a day, propped up on a sofa when he should have been in bed. Warburg admitted that his failure to find Orwell a typist caused the writer to break down and was 'very much on my conscience' and 'disastrous'. Why didn't Orwell simply return to London and have the job done there? Tosco Fyvel put this question to Sonia Orwell (*née* Brownell), who told him:

Oh, George was perfectly aware that he could come to London and engage an efficient secretary, but as he saw things, leaving Jura was just not on. It would have meant an upheaval in his whole consciousness of himself which he did not want to face. Besides, all his life he had ignored his illnesses up to the point where they got too bad, when he went to bed and waited to recover as he always did. Perhaps he thought that this time, too, he would recover; or he just refused to think.

Completing *Nineteen Eighty-Four* had come close to killing Orwell, and he warned that he would look like a 'deaths-head' in any publicity photographs for the book. He realised that he should have been in a sanatorium two months earlier but, he told Fred Warburg: 'I wanted to get that bloody book finished.' The great self-reliant stoic even admitted to Avril: 'Whatever I do, it seems my temperature rises if I take the slightest action or motion.' December saw Orwell confined to bed, and he agreed that he should once more enter a sanatorium. He believed that he would have to go private, as he was too ill to go on a waiting list and wanted to be sure to get his own room where he could write. 'I have a stunning idea for a very short novel,' he told his publisher. His specialist, Dr Dick, had recommended the Grampian Sanatorium at Kingussie, but that didn't have an available room and Orwell was booked into one in the Cotswolds. On Christmas Eve 1948 he wrote his last ever entry in his Jura domestic diary:

Sharp frosts the last two nights. The days sunny & still, sea calm. A(vril) has very bad cold. The goose for Xmas disappeared, then was found swimming in the sea round at the anchorage, about a mile from our own beach. B(ill) thinks it must have swum round. He had to follow it in a dinghy & shoot it. Weight before drawing & plucking, 10½ lbs. Snowdrops up all over the place. A few tulips showing. Some wall-flowers still trying to flower.

On a January evening in 1949 Orwell began the journey that would take him to Cranham sanatorium in Gloucestershire's Cotswold Hills. Orwell, Ricky, Avril and Bill Dunn crammed into Bill Dunn's Austin. Rees recalled: 'Finally, after three years the day came, in January 1949, when I drove him for the last time over the terrible moorland road on the first stage of the long journey to a sanatorium in Gloucestershire.' The pot-hole strewn road to Ardlussa was the most dangerous part of the journey for a very sick man and was not without incident. What followed, however, helped etch the journey into the young mind of five-year-old Ricky Blair:

> I went with him in the back if the car heading down to Ardlussa where he was going to stay for the night in order to catch the steamer the following day. Off we went and the inevitable happened – the car went off the road and his sister my aunt Avril and her husband to be, Bill Dunn, had to walk back to Barnhill to get another vehicle to pull us out. These sort of things happened all the time. It was sort of an everyday occurrence. So he and I, my father and I, sat in the back of the car and he told me little stories. What they were I've no idea. I think he could make up stories as he went along. We just chatted to keep me amused, to while away the time.[26]

Avril recalled: 'It just so happened that, just as the place where the car had got bogged, there was just room, by going well off the road onto the peat bog, to get round the car … and eventually we got a tow-rope on the car and managed to tow it out.' Avril finally got Orwell to Ardlussa, ready to travel to the mainland the next morning. It was the last time Dunn ever saw his future brother-in-law. He remembered him as 'imperturbable, he was terribly calm, and he was always very pleasant. He really was a nice person, very nice, but as I say, I never ever had a very long conversation with him.'

From Hairmyres, Dr Dick wrote to David Astor warning him that his friend would now have to lead a very sheltered life in a sanatorium environment and assuring him that Orwell would be well looked after at Cranham. 'I fear the dream of Jura must fade out,' he added. Orwell's life on his Hebridean island had come to an end, but the island's hold on him had not.

*

In Cranham Sanatorium, Orwell was housed in a small room in a wooden chalet where he was subjected to a regime of fresh air and rest. His door was marked 'Mr. Blair', and staff recalled that there was often confusion when visitors arrived seeking to visit 'Mr. Orwell'. Fred Warburg and his wife visited him and thought the place 'looked more like a sort of Arctic concentration camp than a place where people would get well from TB'.

Orwell deeply missed Barnhill, and although he accepted that he must now endure winters as an invalid, he dreamed of spending summers there. He told Richard Rees: 'Most of my furniture & books are now there, & the garden is more or less under control & could be reorganized so as not to need much doing to it.' Orwell had been uncomfortable that Barnhill farmhouse should be occupied by non-farmers and had been very pleased that Rees had become Bill Dunn's sleeping partner in the farming of Barnhill's fields. He was now afraid that the Rees/Dunn arrangement would fall apart now that he himself wasn't Barnhill's full-time tenant. 'It is very unfortunate that the continued working of the farm more or less depends on our presence, although we are not farmers, & I feel unhappy that my health should interfere with this.' He hoped that Bill would stay on farming at Barnhill, possibly with Avril housekeeping for him or, failing that, Bill living with Tony and

Jeannie Rozga.[27] Even when Bill and Avril announced that they might move to a farm on the mainland, Orwell suggested that – unless the Fletcher family could find a tenant who would farm the land – he might keep the house on as a summer home.

For Orwell, the move from Jura and Scotland to a private sanatorium in the Cotswolds came as a culture shock. The upper-class English accents he heard there appalled him.

Curious effect, here in the sanatorium … of hearing large numbers of upper-class English voices. I have been almost out of the sound of them for two years, hearing them at most one or two at a time, my ears growing more & more used to working-class or lower-middle class Scottish voices. In the hospital at Hairmyres, for instance, I literally never heard a 'cultivated' accent except when I had a visitor. It was as though I was hearing these voices for the first time. And what voices! A sort of over-fedness, a fatuous self-confidence, a constant bah-bahing of laughter about nothing, above all a sort of heaviness and richness combined with a fundamental ill-will – people who, one instinctively feels, without even being able to see them, are the enemies of anything intelligent or sensitive or beautiful. No wonder everyone hates us so.[28]

The voices were jarringly different from the ones he had heard every day on Jura and at Hairmyres Hospital. Tosco Fyvel wrote: 'I think he also liked listening to the soft Scottish working-class speech of his fellow-patients; his early prejudice against all things Scottish and long since disappeared and the patients were for him of the right class.'[29] Who would have guessed that the Old Etonian who once called Scots 'Scotch' – just to annoy them – would come to prefer the accents of the Jura crofters and the staff and patients at Hairmyres hospital to those of his own nationality and class.

More than two months after saying goodbye to Ricky on Jura, Orwell was fretting that the boy was growing away from him and, unable to understand illness, thought of him as someone who was always lying down and couldn't play. But the child's visits posed a health threat to the five-year-old. Orwell's sputum was TB-positive and highly contagious, and he drank and ate from heavy white china that was boiled after every use.

That summer, Avril took Richard down to see his father, lodging the child with friends of Orwell's who lived at the nearby Whiteway anarchist colony. Orwell told Sonia Brownell that Richard attended kindergarten there in the mornings and sometimes visited him in the afternoon. Richard recalled these visits:

When I went to see him at Cranham I would say 'where does it hurt daddy', so I was looking for some physical manifestation of his pain and illness and of course it was internal, and you couldn't see it. It probably didn't occur to me that he was becoming more cadaverous as time went on, so it mystified me and presumably my thoughts wandered off somewhere else. Sadly, I didn't realise how ill he really was.[30]

The nurse in charge of Orwell's ward was Audrey Dawson:

He showed a lot of enthusiasm when his little boy came. He seemed quite excited at the thought of him coming. But I don't think that the boy would have been allowed in regularly, because of his condition. It was a special concession, and he would have been told not to kiss his child. The tubercle is transmitted through the sputum in the breath. The child wouldn't have been allowed to sit on the bed or get too close.[31]

Lettice Cooper recalled that Orwell was terrified that five-year-old Ricky would catch TB and wouldn't let him sit on his knee, even pushing him abruptly away when the child got too close. Orwell's niece Jane and her father Humphrey Dakin also visited, and Jane was horrified to see how ill, cadaverous and worn her uncle looked. David Astor was a regular visitor, as the sanatorium lay between Astor's home and his office at *The Observer*. Astor recalled: 'He was always talking of the things he was going to do. He said to me casually, "Do you think one can die if one has a book in one's mind one wants to write?" I was taken aback. I couldn't imagine the answer.'[32] Orwell went on to admit to Astor that a doctor had told him that, yes, it was possible to die with an unwritten book inside one's head.

CHAPTER 11

1984: As Autobiography

*'The truly frightening thing was the emaciation of his body.
The barrel of the ribs was as narrow as that of a skeleton: the
legs had shrunk so that the knees were thicker than the thighs
… at a guess he would have said that it was the body of a man
of sixty, suffering from some malignant disease.'*

—George Orwell, *Nineteen Eighty-Four*, 1949

Sitting up in his hospital bed, dressed in an old camel-coloured woollen cardigan, Orwell corrected the proofs of the fruits of his Jura labours, and *Nineteen Eighty-Four* was finally published in Britain on 8 June 1949, in the USA five days later, and then quickly re-issued by the American Book of the Month Club. Orwell had tussled with the club, which had wanted to cut two sections from the novel – the text of 'The Theory and Practice of Oligarchical Collectivism', the book supposedly written by the state's principal enemy, Emmanuel Goldstein, and the appendix 'The Principles of Newspeak', a seemingly academic essay that (for those to care to read it) casts a very different light on the book's conclusion.

When Orwell typed 'The End' at the foot of his manuscript, it was wasn't; 'The Principles of Newspeak' forms the end of the book. You can understand why the editors of the American edition wanted this removed. At first glance it seems to be the author simply explaining to the diligent reader that he had clearly thought through how Newspeak might have been developed by the Inner Party to further enslave the population. But readers who persevere with the essay soon realise that it is written in 'Oldspeak', or standard English, and refers to Newspeak entirely in the past tense. We are therefore reading about Newspeak as history. Clearly the boast of Syme, the lexicographer compiling the Newspeak dictionary – that Oldspeak would be extinct by 2050 – has not come to pass. And if Newspeak has failed, have the Thought Police, Oceania and Big Brother himself also failed? Have the proles – who had never had Newspeak inflicted on them and therefore retained the possibility of independent thought – risen and overthrown the regime and perhaps the whole world order? Orwell doesn't tell us – but he offers us hope. He insisted that American readers shared this hope, and 'The Principles of Newspeak' continues to appear in all US editions, while Canadian novelist Margaret Atwood threw readers a similar lifeline of hope in the epilogue of her classic *The Handmaid's Tale*. As Orwell reminded us, *Nineteen Eighty-Four* is a warning, not a prediction.

Sales of *Nineteen Eighty-Four* were phenomenal. Within a year it had sold nearly 50,000 copies in Britain, 170,000 in the US, and yet another 190,000 in the Book of the Month Club edition. Orwell wrote to Julian Symons thanking him for his 'brilliant as well as generous review' in the *Times Literary Supplement* but was less impressed by some American reactions to it, complaining that some Republican newspapers had tried to use the book as propaganda against the Labour Party. Orwell felt too unwell to endure a bed-side interview for *Life* magazine but penned a robust reply which was published in *Life* and the *New York Times Book Review*: 'My recent novel is NOT intended as an attack on Socialism or on the British Labour Party (of which I am a supporter) but as a show-up of the perversions to which a centralized economy is liable and which have already been partly realized in Communism and Fascism ...'

*

Orwell began *Nineteen Eighty-Four* with a famously straightforward but unsettling sentence. Clocks were a device he had used before, and it worked for him again. It was 'about a quarter to eight' on a beastly January morning when George Bowling jumped out of bed and into the first paragraph of *Coming Up for Air*, and 'half past eight' on a sultry April morning when *Burmese Days* opens. *A Clergyman's Daughter* opens with Dorothy Hare being wrenched from sleep by an alarm clock which 'exploded like a horrid little bomb', and 'The clock struck half past two' when we first visit the little bookshop where *Keep the Aspidistra Flying* opens. Four out of five of Orwell's previous novels had begun with time-checks or rude alarms in the first paragraph, jolting the reader to attention and setting the time of the events that would follow before identifying their place. Sitting before his Remington typewriter in a smoke-filled upstairs bedroom at Barnhill farmhouse, Orwell employed that trope again, but this time with a new and unsettling riff that hints of science-fiction: 'It was a bright cold day in April, and the clocks were striking thirteen.'

Four of his five previous novels had been traditional and realistic, set in recognisable times and places. His fifth, *Animal Farm*, he had subtitled 'A Fairy Story' and had gone far beyond realism. With the thirteenth strike of the clocks, Orwell was signalling to his readers that once again he was taking them somewhere strange and beyond their experience.

Nineteen Eighty-Four was very different to Orwell's previous book, but although they are stylistically miles apart, the grim new novel can be seen as a thematic sequel to the 'fairy story' of *Animal Farm*. In *Animal Farm* Orwell told of a revolution betrayed – as he himself had seen in Barcelona. In *Nineteen Eighty-Four* he followed that betrayal to its hideous conclusion, although the grimness of the lives portrayed in his two great anti-totalitarian novels is shot through with satire and black humour. The gallows humour of:

1984: As Autobiography

ALL ANIMALS ARE EQUAL
BUT SOME ANIMALS ARE
MORE EQUAL THAN OTHERS

… allows the *more* equal animals to insist that:

WAR IS PEACE
FREEDOM IS SLAVERY
IGNORANCE IS STRENGTH

Orwell's *Nineteen Eighty-Four* world is a planet carved up by three totalitarian superstates – Eurasia, Eastasia and Oceania – the writer's predicted evolutions of the Soviet Union, China and an American-dominated West. Britain, now designated as Airstrip One, has been subsumed into Oceania and governed by INGSOC, a name derived from 'English Socialism' that implies that the dictatorship is a result of a leftist revolution gone wrong. The most extreme example of an Oceania-style state today is North Korea, which comes complete with its own Big Brother in Kim Jong-un, who must be worshipped and obeyed and whose whim is law.

Orwell doesn't tell INGSOC's back-story of how it came to power in Airstrip One but, given his own experience of seeing the revolution in Barcelona destabilised and betrayed by the Soviet Union's goons, it seems likely that a popular rising in Oceania was railroaded by the Inner Party, which then established the totalitarian regime to consolidate and maintain their power forever. Winston's tormentor O'Brien explains: 'Power is not a means, it is an end. One does not establish a dictatorship in order to safeguard a revolution; one makes the revolution in order to establish the dictatorship. The object of persecution is persecution. The object of torture is torture. The object of power is power. Now do you begin to understand me?'

Society is rigidly and ruthlessly divided into the Inner Party, the Outer Party and the proles. The Inner Party, a Soviet-style *nomenklatura*, is an elite cast with power and privilege that makes up less than two per cent of the population. Winston Smith is astonished at the Inner Party luxuries his lover Julia manages to secure for them:

'It's coffee,' he murmured, 'real coffee.'
'It's Inner Party coffee. There's a whole kilo here,' she said.
'How did you manage to get hold of all these things?'
'It's all Inner Party stuff. There's nothing those swine don't have, nothing.'

Winston Smith belongs to the Outer Party, a class of petty officials constantly snooped on by telescreens – two-way monitors that pump out propaganda while spying on individuals for any sign of political or social deviation. Outer Party members are relentlessly and ruthlessly controlled by the Thought Police: 'In the vast majority of cases there was no trial, no report of the arrest. People simply disappeared, always during the night. Your name was removed from the registers, every record of everything you had ever done was wiped out, your one-time existence was denied and then forgotten. You were abolished, annihilated: *vaporized* was the usual word.'

The proles are the underclass, the lumpenproletariat, the sweated labour and cannon fodder, natural inferiors who are fed cheap gin and pornography to keep them pliant and docile. In the Ministry of Truth's grim canteen, Winston Smith hears his colleague Syme gloat that by 2050 not a single 'human being' would be able to understand anything not spoken in Newspeak. Smith is briefly puzzled:

It had been on the tip of his tongue to say 'Except the proles,' but he checked himself, not feeling fully certain that this remark was not in some way unorthodox. Syme, however, had divined what he was about to say.

'The proles are not human beings,' he said carelessly.

Oceania is a land without God, but its mysterious leader Big Brother fulfils that omniscient role, and – even though he may not actually exist – his rule is ruthlessly enforced. This is the situation Winston Smith finds himself on that that bright cold day in April 1984, as the clock strikes thirteen. There is no glimmer of glasnost, no prospect of perestroika; Inner Party member O'Brien tells Winston: 'If you want a picture of the future, imagine a boot stamping on a human face – for ever.'

Working mostly in his upstairs bedroom at Barnhill, Orwell distilled his memories, experiences, observations, reasoning and fear into his novel. The landscape of *Nineteen Eighty-Four* was a riff on the London of 1948 – the bombed-out landscape, the scarcity of cigarettes and razor blades, the tasteless ersatz food, the grey atmosphere of life in general. The convoy of Eurasian prisoners, 'little yellow men in shabby greenish uniforms' that Winston witnesses squatting in trucks as they pass through Victory Square, have their origins in 'the wretched prisoners squatting in their reeking cages' that Orwell recalled from his Burmese police days in *The Road to Wigan Pier*. The hapless proles of Airstrip One resemble the desperately deprived figures his readers encountered in *Down and Out in Paris and London* and *The Road to Wigan Pier*.

The Two Minutes Hate scene in *Nineteen Eighty-Four* – where citizens are encouraged show their loathing for supposed enemies – has likely roots in the British Union of Fascists meeting that Orwell attended to hear its leader Oswald Mosley speak. Mosley had been accompanied by about a hundred uniformed Blackshirts, who violently ejected dissenters while Mosley whipped up his audience against easy scapegoats, Jews and foreigners. Orwell left Barnsley Town Hall lamenting 'how easy it is to bamboozle an uneducated audience ...'.

Winston's persecutor, O'Brien, has an Irish/Catholic name, and perhaps represents Orwell's long-held view that the Catholic Church was pro-fascist. The dismal BBC wartime canteen that Orwell knew during his propaganda years became that of Outer Party propaganda apparatchiks like Winston Smith. The blueprint of the Ministry of Truth's 'enormous pyramidal structure of glittering white concrete' was the 1930s art deco Senate building in Bloomsbury where Eileen worked for the Press and Censorship Bureau of the Ministry of Information.

David Astor speculated that treatments Orwell received in hospital were the basis for Winston's torture, and details of actual torture would have come from his friend Georges Kopp who had experienced eighteen months of terrifying NKVD hospitality in Barcelona. Winston and Julia conduct their euphoric love affair in a little bedroom above a chaotic shop – the very setting for Orwell and Eileen's blissful first six months of marriage. Even Winston Smith's physical health echo Orwell's own and the writer didn't have to go further than his own bedroom to find the inspiration for Winston Smith being 'doubled up by a violent coughing fit which nearly always attacked him soon after waking up. It emptied his lungs so completely that he could only begin breathing again by lying on his back and taking a series of deep gasps.'

Orwell has Winston born in 1934 or '35 (Winston isn't sure), but if it was1934, then he was born in the same year as Orwell's son Richard, making the great dystopian novel as much personal as political. Writer Thomas Pynchon finds it 'not difficult to guess that Orwell was imagining a future for his son's generation, a world that he was wishing upon them as warning against'.[1]

Orwell – under surveillance by British Intelligence since he had begun work on *The Road to Wigan Pier* – had long feared the imposition of a surveillance society, a preoccupation at the root of the telescreens of Big Brother and evident in his work since he wrote *The Lion and the Unicorn* in 1941: 'The most hateful of all names in an English ear is Nosey Parker. It is obvious, of course, that even this purely private liberty is a lost cause. Like all other modern peoples, the English are in the process of being numbered, labelled, conscripted, "co-ordinated".'

For Orwell, truth was sacred, but he harboured 'the feeling that the very concept of objective truth is fading out of the world' and pondered the likelihood of the public falling for a Big Brother's fantastic lies the way people had fallen for Stalin's in Spain.[2] In 1940 he had reviewed American social psychologist Hadley Cantril's book *The Invasion from Mars*. The book explored the panic caused on Halloween 1938 by Orson Welles's radio version of H.G. Wells's *The War of the Worlds*. It is thought that up to a million of the drama's six million listeners believed it to be a news report and thousands fled from their homes in panic. Orwell reflected: 'The truly astonishing thing, however, was that so few of the listeners attempted any kind of check.' Cantril discovered that those taken in by Welles's drama were mostly the poor, ill-educated, economically insecure and those with unhappy private lives. Orwell concluded:

The evident connection between personal unhappiness and readiness to believe the incredible is its most interesting discovery. Remarks like 'Everything is so upset in the world that anything might happen,' or 'So long as everybody was going to die, it was all right,' are surprisingly common in the answers to the questionnaire. People who have been out of work or on the verge of bankruptcy for ten years may be actually relieved to hear of the approaching end of civilisation. It is a similar frame of mind that has induced whole nations to fling themselves into the arms of a Saviour.[3]

In his 1946 essay *The Prevention of Literature* Orwell had warned: 'From the totalitarian point of view history is something to be created rather than learned.' In *Nineteen Eighty-Four* that has become a party slogan: 'Who controls the past controls the future. Who controls the present controls the past.' Inconvenient facts in Airstrip One can be disposed of in 'memory holes' where they are incinerated, the past can be rewritten and people be coerced into believing what tangible evidence told them was false. In Spain Orwell had looked around and seen doublethink at work: 'If the Leaders says of such and such an event, "It never happened" – well, it never happened. If he says two and two are five, well two and two are five.'[4]

In January 2017 Kellyanne Conway, the Senior Counselor to President Donald Trump, brought Orwell's doublethink into sharp focus when citing 'alternative facts' to explain why the new president claimed a record turn-out for his inauguration when video and photographic evidence proved otherwise. 'Look,' challenged American television's *Meet the Press* interviewer Chuck Todd, 'alternative facts are not facts. They're falsehoods.' The following month, in defence of Trump's ban on immigration, Conway quoted 'alternative facts' again when she inflated what was probably the arrest six years previously of two Iraqi refugees in Bowling Green, Kentucky, into 'the Bowling Green massacre' – a terrorist outrage that never happened. Fortunately, the American press was able to disprove and ridicule Conway's claims, but the threat of the rich and powerful being free to use mass media to make up and repeat totally bogus claims to falsify public consciousness is terrifying. On a positive note, the US sales of *Nineteen Eighty-Four* increased ninety-five-fold, making it Amazon's number-one bestseller for a time.

Closer to home, Dominic Cummings, for sixteen months chief adviser to Prime Minister Boris Johnson, claimed that he had written warning about the 'threat of coronaviruses' the year before Covid-19 rampaged around the world. He had not. It emerged that he had re-written his blog – attempted to alter history – after the virus struck, in order to back up his false claim of foresight. Cummings was rumbled, but on Airstrip One, where all media is party media, Winston Smith realises that the past 'had not merely been altered, it had actually been destroyed. For how could you establish even the most obvious fact when there existed no record outside your own memory?'

In the twenty-first century there is no need for INGSOC's formally constituted Ministry of Truth. Bots, troll factories, media ownership by a clique of super-rich, the sycophancy of client media, disinformation, fake news and hate speech all conspire to do the ministry's work for it. Typing in that fume-reeking little room at Barnhill, Orwell warned us. We would do well to listen to him.

CHAPTER 12

Final Chapter

'I am afraid of death. You are young, so presumably you're more afraid of it than I am. Obviously we shall put it off as long as we can. But it makes very little difference. So long as human beings stay human, death and life are the same thing.'

—Winston to Julia. George Orwell,
Nineteen Eighty-Four, 1949

In late August 1949, when it became clear that *Nineteen Eighty-Four* was a success, Orwell wrote to his publisher Fred Warburg with news: 'I intend getting married again (to Sonia) when I am once again in the land of the living, if I ever am. I suppose everyone will be horrified, but apart from other considerations I really think I should stay alive longer if I were married.'

Orwell had been attracted to Sonia Brownell for a long time, having met her in 1940 at the offices of Cyril Connolly's *Horizon*, where she worked as a literary assistant. Sonia had been one of the women the lonely writer had proposed to shortly after Eileen's death and, although she may have slept with Orwell, had refused marriage and never took up the offer of visiting him on Jura. Now she accepted the successful but ailing author's proposal.

In early September Orwell became seriously ill and was transferred to Room 65 in the private wing of University College Hospital, London. The dedicated, indeed compulsive, writer was now silenced. Lying incapacitated in hospital must have been depressing for the workaholic. He wrote: 'Throughout that time there has literally not been one day in which I did not feel that I was idling, that I was behind with the current job, & that my total output was miserably small. Even at the periods when I was working 10 hours a day on a book, or turning out 4 or 5 articles a week, I never have been able to get away from this neurotic feeling, that I was wasting my time.'[1]

Whenever Orwell completed a book, he was always haunted by the possibility that there would never be another one. Fearing that this might now come true, he wrote to Philip Rahv, the co-founder of the influential American literary magazine *Partisan Review*: 'I have hardly set pen to paper since last December.' Yet his letter reveals hopes of recovery: 'This beastly disease (T.B.) works very slowly, & although I am supposed to be getting on fairly well it is possible that I shall be incapacitated for the better part of another year.' He thought he would travel abroad for the sake of his health and asked his agent to keep any money from the French translation of *Nineteen Eighty-Four* in France so that he would have a source of foreign currency.

Avril and Richard were now back on Jura, where Richard had started at the village school in Inverlussa, a mile from Ardlussa. Richard told the *Orwell Society* in 2012: 'I would go down on the boat on a Monday morning and come home on the Friday afternoon. During the week I stayed with the postmaster and his wife. I don't recall being homesick so I must have been well looked after.'

Orwell thought Richard a bit backward in talking, but lively and fascinated with farming and boats. 'I shan't influence him if I can help it,' Orwell said, 'but if he does grow up to be a farmer, a sailor, a civil engineer or something useful of that description I should be very pleased.' Ricky did not disappoint. He left school to attend agricultural colleges and then went on to work for Massey Ferguson, the agricultural machinery company, before founding a tourist business in Argyll.

On 13 October 1949 Orwell's bizarre second wedding was held, an occasion that David Astor found 'embarrassing'. The groom sat up in bed in his tiny hospital room wearing a cerise smoking jacket bought for the occasion. The guests were Janetta Woolley, a literary-set girlfriend of Sonia's and her journalist husband Robert Kee, a hospital doctor, the chaplain and best man David Astor, who thought that Orwell was just skin and bone and looked like Gandhi. Orwell's description of Winston Smith before he is finally broken in Room 101 could have been autobiography:

> But the truly frightening thing was the emaciation of his body. The barrel of the ribs was as narrow as that of a skeleton: the legs had shrunk so that the knees were thicker than the thighs. He saw now what O'Brien had meant about seeing the side view. The curvature of the spine was astonishing. The thin shoulders were hunched forward so as to make a cavity of the chest, the scraggy neck seemed to be bending double under the weight of the skull. At a guess he would have said that it was the body of a man of sixty, suffering from some malignant disease.

After the simple wedding ceremony, Orwell remained in bed while the others trooped off for lunch at the Ritz. Astor recalled: 'Sonia was a very handsome, fine-looking, delightful person. In *Nineteen Eighty-Four* there's a girl called Julia who seems too good to be true; she never becomes a real person. I think he saw Sonia that way. Eileen was his workaday wife; Sonia was an idealised female he dreamt of. He thought to keep alive he must marry her. It was a gesture to say he wasn't going to die.'[2]

In January 1950 Avril took Richard to London to see his father and spent a week or so there. Orwell was only days from being flown to a Swiss sanatorium and was so convinced that he would get better there that his fishing rods lay propped in a corner of his room, ready for the journey. Only six months previously he had confided to Fred Warburg that he hoped people would not badger him about going to Switzerland with its supposed magical qualities. 'I don't believe it makes any difference where you are, & a journey would be the death of me,' he had written. But David Astor recalled that Sonia thought her husband would get better: 'I don't think she thought he was dying. I'm sure she didn't from what she said to me. I think both of them were acting in some sort of fantasy way.'[3]

The poet Stephen Spender believed that Orwell was very much in love with Sonia and, while Sonia was fond of him, she 'always wanted to have a genius in her life. She had a romantic conception of genius. Orwell, to some extent, fitted her idea of the solitary genius who needed backing. She was always in search of her genius.' Spender dismissed any accusation that she married the ailing Orwell for money as 'totally unjust'. And Avril Blair told Bernard Crick that she felt that Sonia was a 'fame hunter' not a gold digger.

In *Nineteen Eighty-Four* Orwell has Winston muse over his affair with Julia: 'It was impossible that this affair should end successfully; such things did not happen in real life.' One wonders how the relationship with Sonia would have gone if Orwell had recovered sufficiency for him to return to Jura, write the new novels he had planned and raise his son there. The soirée-loving Sonia may not have thrived on rainswept and rugged Jura, and of the many people who knew her and wrote or talked to biographers about her, none have used the word 'maternal'. Sonia Brownell/Orwell was not cut out to be a Hebridean mother and smallholder or, as Richard Blair put it: 'Sonia wasn't designed to go roaming in the gloaming in big boots and hairy socks.'[4] While Sonia was Richard's legal stepmother, it was Aunt Avril who raised him. 'There is no doubt that Av treated me as her own. There was certainly a bond between us.'

Sonia and Orwell placed a lot of hope on the Swiss sanatorium, but Howard Nicholson, a junior chest doctor at the hospital, told CBC: 'It was put across that it was a good thing to be in a higher altitude, with pure air, but really I don't think that it made the least difference. I think it was mainly a method of letting the patients die comfortably, in a place where they were really used to dealing with that sort of thing.'[5]

Orwell was devoid of self-pity and made no mention of death to visiting friends like Tosco Fyvel, who found visits to the writer's bedside melancholy but never depressing. While Orwell's body may have been wasted, his mind was alert and he kept up on news, politics and culture. Fyvel says Orwell's mind was 'stocked with projects', including a three-volume work that some biographers have suggested akin to Thomas Mann's multi-generational saga *Buddenbrooks*.

A few days after his marriage, Orwell was visited by his friend Rayner Heppenstall: 'Orwell was in a private room with his own telephone, at University College Hospital. He apologised for this grandeur. The last opinion I heard him enunciate was that, whereas formerly he had always derided attempts to preserve archaic languages like Welsh and Gaelic, he now thought such attempts worth supporting.'[6]

It seems that Jura, with its majority of Gaelic speakers, had worked their magic on Orwell. Bernard Crick suggests: 'Perhaps his English patriotism was at last trying to come to terms with a broader concept of the United Kingdom and its nations.'

Paul Potts, whose friendship with Orwell had continued despite being driven from Barnhill by the cold shoulders of Avril and Susan Watson, is likely to have been the last person to see the writer alive. Orwell had worried about getting proper Ceylon tea in Switzerland rather than 'that filthy China stuff', and Potts had brought him a pack as a parting gift. 'Tea was rationed then, so I'd brought him some. There was a window in the door and you could look in, and I saw he was asleep, and I knew he had a great deal of difficulty in getting to sleep, so I didn't wake him up, and I left the tea at the door. But he died just after that. I often wonder who got the tea.'

Orwell died alone that night of a massive haemorrhage of the lung; he bled to death. Dr James Williamson, who had treated Orwell, concluded: 'He didn't actually die of consumption in the classical sense, he died of a complication, you might say, he died of a blood vessel becoming eroded and there was no way of stopping that.'[7]

In the morning, the BBC broadcast the news of Orwell's death, which was heard at Barnhill by Avril Blair and the little boy she and her soon-to-be husband would now bring up as their own. Richard and Avril had been at the writer's bedside less than a week before. 'It has been said that my brother really didn't want to go on living,' she recalled. 'I didn't form that impression. I remember him saying to me once that he wanted to live at least until young Richard was fourteen.'[8] Avril had hardly time to unpack at Barnhill before it was time to leave again for London and her brother's funeral.

Orwell, the confirmed atheist but lover of English tradition was buried – as he had been first married – according to the ritual of the Church of England. David Astor recalled that when he and Avril Blair left the churchyard, he had asked her who or what sort of person he had most admired:

She just turned to me and said quite easily and directly, 'The working-class mother of ten children.' It took me by surprise, because I wasn't expecting that as an answer. But the more you think about it, the more true it was. And I think he meant the ordinary person's capacity to deal with lots of problems and to deal with them successfully, to manage. And I think he revered ordinary people in a sensible way, and not in some falsely romantic way.

It was such ordinary people on Jura – the farmers, fishermen, estate workers and tradesmen – that had quietly impressed Orwell and swept away his long held anti-Scottish prejudice. The future, believed Orwell, belonged to such people who, realising their strength, would raise their consciousness and change the world for the betterment of humanity. That was the glimmer of hope that penetrated the dark world of *Nineteen Eighty-Four*: 'The future belonged to the proles. And could he be sure that when their time came the world they constructed would not be just as alien to him, Winston Smith, as the world of the Party? Yes, because at the least it would be a world of sanity. Where there is equality there can be sanity. Sooner or later it would happen, strength would change into consciousness.'

Less than two weeks after Orwell's funeral – and with impeccable timing – the Communist German Democratic Republic founded the Stasi – its secret police, its Thought Police, its Big Brother. With the motto 'Shield and Sword of the Party', and the goal of perpetual power, it quickly outstripped Nazi Germany's Gestapo in its might and all-pervasiveness. In 1941 the Gestapo held all of Germany, Austria and what is now the Czech Republic in its grip with fewer than 15,000 officers. Prior to German unification in 1990, the Stasi had 90,000 professional goons along with a network of 110,000 civilian informers, narks and toadies in its paranoid mission to control just East Germany.[9] Spouses betrayed each other. Old friends turned Judas. Children denounced parents. It would have been no surprise to Orwell, or to Winston Smith's neighbour Tom Parsons whose own daughter betrays him to the Thought Police:

All their ferocity was turned outwards, against the enemies of the State, against foreigners, traitors, saboteurs, thought-criminals. It was almost normal for people over thirty to be frightened of their own children. And with good reason, for hardly a week passed in which *The Times* did not carry a paragraph describing how some eavesdropping little sneak – 'child hero' was the phrase generally used – had overheard some compromising remark and denounced its parents to the Thought Police.[10]

In the autumn of 1950, Bill Dunn, Avril and Richard left Barnhill and Jura; Bill to stay with a friend until he found a new farm, and Avril and Richard to the home of her brother-in-law Humphrey Dakin. The following year, Avril and Bill got married and, together with Richard, moved into Gartcharron, a hill farm by Loch Craignish only four or five miles as the crow flies from Barnhill. Richard lived on the farm until it was time for him to go to senior school. That school, albeit a private one, was in Scotland. His aunt Avril had married a Scots farmer. Ricky bore a Scots Gaelic name and learned to play the bagpipes. The son of a very English writer had come home to the land of the Blairs.

And so, to the 'what ifs?' What if Orwell had not had an allergic reaction to the Streptomycin? What if the drug had cured him and allowed him to return to Jura to write? Would we now have the short novel based on the 'stunning idea' he had told his publisher Fred Warburg about? Would we have the three-volume *Buddenbrooks*-style work that he hinted about to Tosco Fyvel? Would we have a raft of insightful journalism in which he began to ponder 'whither Scotland?' Might George Orwell's later years have given us a distinctive 'Jura period' body of work?

It is fun, but fruitless to speculate. However, if readers will indulge me, I can't help wondering – might this lover of words, and able linguist capable of learning Burmese, Hindustani and S'gaw-Karen, have been inspired by his new-found sympathy for Gaelic and his neighbours who spoke it to learn some of that language?

Might he have learned to respond to the question '*Ciamar a tha sibh?*' (How are you?) with '*Tha gu math*' (I am well)?

In that speculative spirit, I close with:

Is cogadh sìth – War is peace
Is saorsa braighdeanas – Freedom is slavery
Is aineolas neart – Ignorance is strength

AFTERWORD

As I was writing this book, Vladimir Putin launched his merciless invasion of Ukraine. After the slaughter in Russian-occupied areas, surviving Ukrainian community leaders were arrested, children deported to be fostered in Russia, museums looted and books in the Ukrainian language burned. Russian was to become conquered Ukraine's Newspeak. The language of resistance was to be first impoverished and then silenced, exactly as done by Big Brother's Ministry of Truth in Winston Smith's world. 'War' never quite became 'Peace' – but it did become 'Special Military Operations' in Putin's twisted doublethink.

A handful of fascist-leaning dictatorships (Big Brother's Little Brothers) supported the Russian aggressor, but in the West NATO rediscovered its purpose and Britain and the European Union found common cause. Sweden and Finland defied the totalitarian state on their borders and applied for NATO membership. Meanwhile, China flexed its muscles by mounting massive and intimidating military exercises off the coast of Taiwan, a Western-style democracy. Nearly eighty years on from Orwell's *Nineteen Eighty-Four*, the dystopian world order of Eurasia, Oceania and Eastasia seemed more like current affairs than literary history.

As I look at my bookshelves, burgeoning with works by or about Orwell, I derive some comfort in the fact that, yes, in our terrifying age there probably *is* room for *another* biography about a man who believed in the human potential for kindness and decency, who gives the idea of democratic socialism a good name and lived by his principles. 'Those are my principles, and if you don't like them … well, I have others.' It is a line attributed to Marx – Groucho, not Karl – and it neatly skewers the kind of person who has no principles. But changing principles is very different from not having them. Before going to fight in Spain, and during his time there, Orwell seriously considered joining the communist-led International Brigade, but his harrowing experience in Barcelona turned him into a passionate anti-communist – a difficult position for a man of the left to hold during Britain's wartime love affair with Stalin. As Orwell wrote in the preface to the 1947 Ukrainian edition of *Animal Farm*: 'These man-hunts in Spain went on at the same time as the great purges in the USSR ... to experience all this was a valuable object lesson: it taught me how easily totalitarian propaganda can control the opinion of enlightened people in democratic countries.'

Prior to the second World War, Orwell saw possible conflict with Germany as an imperialist/capitalist war to be resisted at all costs. But, at the outbreak of hostilities, he was desperate to fight for his country. It was 'a terrible blow' to him being unable to enlist but he 'did his bit' in the Home Guard and as a BBC propagandist.[1]

Orwell was also prepared to change his mind about people. On one occasion he denounced poet Stephen Spender in print as a 'parlor Bolshie'. Orwell was generally homophobic, often using the insults 'nancy' and 'pansy', and Spender was not only a devout communist but also had homosexual as well as heterosexual affairs. And then the two men met. They became friends with Orwell admitting to Spender:

I have been very hostile to the C.P. [Communist Party] since about 1935, &c. because not having met you I could regard you as a type & also an abstraction. Even if when I met you I had not happened to like you, I should still have been bound to change my attitude, because when you meet anyone in the flesh you realize immediately that he is a human being & not a sort of caricature embodying certain ideas.[2]

AFTERWORD

As with Spender, so with Scots. It was getting to know people 'in the flesh' on Jura and at Hairmyres Hospital, rather than 'the millionaires with their Scottish castles' and the racist club bores in Burma that he had previously endured, that wrought the change in Orwell's mind and heart. The Diùraich were ordinary folk trying their hardest to make decent lives for themselves and their families, not 'types', 'abstractions' or 'caricatures', but human beings. The writing of *Nineteen Eighty-Four* on Jura ran parallel to the vanquishing of a long-held prejudice. The 'odious little snob',[3] as Orwell described his teenage self, had never stopped confronting the bigotry and preconceptions of his class, race and age. In the words of Orwell scholar Douglas Kerr: 'All Orwell's career was a struggle to stop being the person he was, and to become someone better.'[4]

As a Scottish admirer of Orwell, the defeat of his anti-Scots prejudice is of some satisfaction to me, but the greatest triumph of his Jura years is the masterpiece he wrote there. Many readers have found *Nineteen Eighty-Four* a grim, depressing read – perhaps all the more so because it horrifyingly reminds us of events and ideologies infesting our world today. But Orwell's dystopian science-fiction is not a prediction; it is a warning. The totalitarian impulse that Orwell feared never sleeps. Today, many people are living lives not far removed from the tyranny depicted in *Nineteen Eighty-Four* and progressive people in the democratic West find ourselves in ideological trenches on the frontline against it. Orwell wrote:

> The scene of the book is laid in Britain in order to emphasise that the English-speaking races are not innately better than anyone else and that totalitarianism, *if not fought against*, could triumph anywhere.[5]

We have been warned.

Endnotes

INTRODUCTION

1. Audrey Coppard & Bernard Crick, *Orwell Remembered*, Aerial Books/BBC, 1984.

2. George Orwell, Letter to George Woodcock, 2nd September 1946.

3. Christopher Hitchens, Address to the Commonwealth Club, California, 21st October 2002.

CHAPTER 1

1. Bernard Crick, introduction to *The Lion and the Unicorn*, Penguin, 1982; Peter Stansky and William Abrahams, *The Unknown Orwell*, Constable, 1972; Rebecca Solnit, *Orwell's Roses*, Granta 2021; Edward M. Thomas, *Orwell*, Writers & Critics series, Oliver & Boyd, 1965.

2. Richard Rees, *George Orwell: Fugitive from the Camp of Victory*, Secker & Warburg, 1961.

3. Stephen Wadhams, *The Orwell Tapes*, Locarno Press, 2017.

4. Audrey Coppard & Bernard Crick, *Orwell Remembered*, Aerial Books/BBC, 1984.

5. Richard Bradford, *Orwell: A Man of our Time*, Bloomsbury Caravel, 2020.

6. Jeffrey Meyers, *Orwell: The Wintry Conscience of a Generation*, W. W. Norton, 2000.

7. Tom Devine, *To the Ends of the Earth*, Allan Lane, 2011.

8. Angus Calder, *Scotlands of the Mind*, Luath Press, 2002.

9. Edward Long, *The History of Jamaica*, 1774.

10. Edward Long, *History of Jamaica, vol 2*, 1774.

11. Captain J. Lawrence-Archer, *Monumental Inscriptions of the British West Indies*, 1875.

12. University College London, Centre for the Study of the Legacies of British Slavery, Database, 2020.

13. Catherine Hall, Nicolas Draper, Keith McClelland, Kate Donington, and Rachael Lang, *Legacies of British Slave-Ownership: Colonial Slavery and the Formation of Victorian Britain*, Cambridge University Press, 2014.

14. Les Wilson, *Putting the Tea in Britain: How Scots Made Our National Drink*, Birlinn, 2021.

15. Rudyard Kipling, *In An Opium Factory,* 1888.

16. Charles Bruce, *Report to the East India Company,* quoted in Nathan Allen MD's *The Opium Trade: Including a sketch of its History, Extent, Effects etc. as Carried on in India and China,* 1853.

17. George Orwell, *The Road to Wigan Pier*, Victor Gollancz, 1937.

18. George Orwell, *Such, Such Were the Joys*, Partisan Review, 1952.

19. George Orwell, *Politics vs Literature: An Examination of Gulliver's Travels*, Polemic, 1946.

20. George Orwell, *Such, Such Were the Joys*, Partisan Review, 1952.

21. Peter Stansky & William Abrahams, *The Unknown Orwell,* Constable, 1972.

22. John Hodge, Screenplay for *Trainspotting,* based on the 1993 novel by Irvine Welsh. Directed by Danny Boyle, 1996.

23. Jeffrey Meyers, *Orwell: Wintry Conscience of a Generation*, W. W. Norton & Company, 2000.

CHAPTER 2

1. George Orwell, *The Road to Wigan Pier*, Victor Gollancz, 1937.

2. Rudyard Kipling, *Barrack Room Ballads and Other Verse*, 1892.

3. Michael Fry, *The Scottish Empire*, The Tuckwell Press & Birlinn, 2001.

4. Anthony Powell, *George Orwell*, The Atlantic, 1967.

5. Peter Stansky & William Abrahams, *The Unknown Orwell,* Constable, 1972.

6. George Orwell, The Road to Wigan Pier, Victor Gollancz, 1937.

7. Richard Bradford, *Orwell: A Man Of Our Time*, Bloomsbury Caravel, 2020.

8. George Orwell, *The Road to Wigan Pier*, Victor Gollancz, 1937.

9. George Orwell, *Autobiographical Note*, Twentieth Century Authors, 1942.

10. Although Deputy Commissioner MacGregor has an impeccably

Scottish name, he is described as a 'Fine Old English Gentleman'. The term is used ironically as MacGregor has fathered nine children by native women, none of whom he provides for.

11. George Orwell, *The Road to Wigan Pier*, Victor Gollancz, 1937.

12. George Orwell, *The Road to Wigan Pier*, Victor Gollancz, 1937.

13. Audrey Coppard & Bernard Crick, *Orwell Remembered*, Aerial Books/BBC, 1984.

14. Stephen Wadhams, *The Orwell Tapes*, Locarno Press, 2017.

15. Audrey Coppard & Bernard Crick, *Orwell Remembered*, Aerial Books/BBC, 1984.

16. Stephen Wadhams, *The Orwell Tapes*, Locarno Press, 2017.

17. Avril Blair, interview with Orwell scholar Ian Angus, 1964.

CHAPTER 3

1. George Orwell, Letter to Rayner Heppenstall, 16th April 1940.

2. Edward M. Thomas, *Orwell*, Writers & Critics series, Oliver & Boyd, 1965.

3. Peter Stansky & William Abrahams, *The Unknown Orwell*, Constable, 1972.

4. Stephen Wadhams, *The Orwell Tapes*, Locarno Press, 2017.

5. Stephen Wadhams, *The Orwell Tapes*, Locarno Press, 2017.

6. Bernard Crick, *Orwell: A Life*, Secker & Warburg, 1980.

7. Stephen Wadhams, *The Orwell Tapes*, Locarno Press 2017.

8. George Orwell, Letter to Rayner Heppenstall, 17th July 1944.

9. Jonathan Swift, *The Publick Spirit of the Whigs*, 1714.

10. George Orwell, Letter to Anthony Powell, 8th June 1936.

11. Stephen Wadhams, *The Orwell Tapes*, Locarno Press 2017.

12. Sylvia Topp, *Eileen: The Making of George Orwell*, Unbound, 2020.

13. Sylvia Topp, *Eileen: The Making of George Orwell*, Unbound, 2020.

14. Sylvia Topp, *Eileen: The Making of George Orwell*, Unbound, 2020.

15. George Orwell, Letter to Denys King-Farlow, 9th June 1936.

16. Peter Stansky & William Abrahams, *The Unknown Orwell*, Constable, 1972.

CHAPTER 4

1. George Orwell, *Homage to Catalonia*, Secker & Warburg, 1938.

2. George Orwell, *The Lion and the Unicorn*, Searchlight/Secker & Warburg, 1941.

3. Stephen Wadhams, *The Orwell Tapes*, Locarno Press, 2017.

4. *The Spanish Revolution, Bulletin of the Worker's Party of Marxist Unification P.O.U.M.*, 3rd February 1937, Barcelona.

5. George Orwell, Letter to Eileen Blair, 5th? April 1937.

6. In *The Road to Wigan Pier*, Orwell recalled the time of the coal strikes when a miner was thought of as a fiend incarnate and old ladies looked under their beds every night lest Robert Smillie should be concealed there.

7. George Orwell. Homage to Catalonia, Secker & Warburg, 1938.

8. George Orwell, *Homage to Catalonia*, Secker & Warburg, 1938.

9. Stephen Wadhams, *The Orwell Tapes*, Locarno Press, 2017.

10. Richard Rees, George Orwell: *Fugitive from the Camp of Victory*, Secker & Warburg, 1961.

11. James K. Hopkins, *Into the Heart of the Fire: The British in the Spanish Civil War*, Stanford University Press, 1996.

12. Richard Bradford; *Orwell: A Man of Our Time*, Bloomsbury Caravel, 2020.

13. Christopher Hitchens, *Why Orwell Matters*, Basic Books, 2002.

14. Peter Obourn, *The Assault on Truth*, Simon & Schuster, 2021.

15. George Orwell, *Why I Write*, summer edition, Gangrel, 1946.

16. George Orwell, *Arthur Koestler, Critical Essays*, Secker & Warburg, 1946.

CHAPTER 5

1. George Orwell, Marrakesh, *New Writing*, 1939.

2. George Orwell, *Coming Up For Air*, Victor Gollancz, 1939.

3. George Orwell, Letter to Geoffrey Gorer, 15th September 1937.

4. Anthony Powell, *George Orwell*, The Atlantic, 1967.

5. George Orwell, Letter to Geoffrey Gorer, 10th January 1940.

6. R.H. is probably Rayner Heppenstall, and the story is probably not

true. The first British air raid casualty of the war was James Isbister of Brig O' Waith near Stenness on Mainland, Orkney. The target of the Luftwaffe's raid on 16 March 1940 was the British fleet at Scapa Flow.

7. George Orwell, *Domestic Diary*, 20th June 1940.

8. Sylvia Topp, *Eileen: The Making of George Orwell*, Unbound, 2021.

9. Tosco Fyvel: *George Orwell: A Life*, Weidenfeld & Nicolson, 1982.

10. Sylvia Topp, *Eileen: The Making of George Orwell*, Unbound, 2021.

11. Stephen Wadhams, *The Orwell Tapes*, Locarno Press, 2017.

12. George Orwell, Review, *Time & Tide*, 8th June 1940.

13. *Interview with Julian Symons*, Arena, BBC, 1983.

14. Stephen Wadhams, *The Orwell Tapes*, Locarno Press, 2017.

15. George Orwell, Letter to Editor, *Time and Tide,* 22nd June 1940.

16. George Orwell, Letter to James Laughlin, 16th July 1940.

17. George Orwell, *Wartime Diary*, 3rd July 1941.

18. Constance Markievicz was the first woman elected to the House in 1918, but as a member of Sinn Fein did not take her seat.

19. George Orwell, *Politic v. Literature: An Examination of Gulliver's Travels*, 1946.

20. Stephen Wadhams, *The Orwell Tapes*, Locarno Press, 2017.

21. George Orwell, *Essay: The Prevention of Literature*, Polemic, 1946.

22. Frederic Warburg, *All Authors Are Equal*, Hutchison, 1973.

23. Stephen Wadhams, *The Orwell Tapes*, Locarno Press, 2017.

24. Julian Symons, *Orwell's obituary*, *Tribune*, 1950.

25. George Orwell: *Politics v. Literature: An Examination of Gulliver's Travels*, 1946.

CHAPTER 6

1. George Orwell, Letter to Anne Popham, 18th April 1946, shown to Bernard Crick.

2. Stephen Wadhams, *The Orwell Tapes*, Locarno Press, 2017.

3. Tosco Fyvel, *Orwell: A Personal Memoir*, Weidenfeld & Nicolson, 1982.

4. Tosco Fyvel, *Orwell: A Personal Memoir*, Weidenfeld & Nicolson, 1982.

5. Tosco Fyvel, *Orwell: A Personal Memoir*, Weidenfeld & Nicolson, 1982.

6. Tosco Fyvel, *Orwell: A Personal Memoir*, Weidenfeld & Nicolson, 1982.

7. Rosina Harrison, *Rose: My Life in Service*, Cassell, 1976.

8. Rosina Harrison, *Rose: My Life in Service*, Cassell, 1976.

9. Powell's first choice of location was Colonsay, but the practicalities of feeding and boarding a feature film unit there defeated him, and he shot the movie mostly on Mull.

10. Michael Powell, *A Life in Movies*, Heinemann, 1986.

11. Powell did meet Avril Blair in Lochgilphead later, simply describing her as 'a sturdy girl'.

12. Letter to Leonard Moore, 30th July 1949.

13. Stephen Wadhams, *The Orwell Tapes*, Locarno Press, 2017.

14. George Orwell, Letter to George Woodcock, 9th August 1947.

15. Eileen Blair to George Orwell, 21st March 1945.

16. Gordon Wright, *Jura & George Orwell*, D.G.B. Wright, Isle of Jura, 1993.

17. Tosco Fyvel, *Orwell: A Personal Memoir*, Weidenfeld & Nicolson, 1982.

18. Stephen Wadhams, *The Orwell Tapes*, Locarno Press, 2017.

19. Stephen Wadhams, *The Orwell Tapes*, Locarno Press, 2017.

20. George Orwell, Letter to Anne Popham, 18th April 1946.

21. T.R. Fyvel, *George Orwell: A Personal Memoir*, Weidenfeld & Nicolson, 1982.

22. Audrey Coppard & Bernard Crick, *Orwell Remembered*, Aerial Books/BBC, 1984.

23. George Orwell, Letter to Anne Popham, 28th April 1946.

24. Audrey Coppard & Bernard Crick, *Orwell Remembered*, Ariel Books/BBC, 1984.

25. George Orwell, Letter to Julian Symons, 20th April 1948.

26. George Orwell, Letter to Anne Popham, 18th April 1946, shown to Bernard Crick.

27. Interview with Susan Watson, Arena, BBC, 1983.

Endnotes

28. George Orwell, Letter to Geoffrey Gorer, 22nd January 1946.

29. Interview with Tosco Fyvel, *Arena*, BBC, 1983.

30. At seventeen, Stafford Cottman was the youngest ILP volunteer to fight in the Spanish Civil War. Cottman features in *Homage to Catalonia*, and Ken Loach's film *Land and Freedom* is largely based on Cottman's experiences.

31. George Orwell, Letter to Stafford Cottman, 25th April,1946.

32. Which did not prevent Orwell and Kopp falling out about an old Ford lorry that Kopp sold to Orwell which seemingly never got further than the pier at Craighouse on Jura.

33. Stephen Wadhams, *The Orwell Tapes*, Locarno Press, 2017.

CHAPTER 7

1. Gordon Wright, *Jura & George Orwell*, D.G.B. Wright, Isle of Jura, 1993.

2. Richard Rees, *George Orwell: Fugitive from the Camp of Victory*, Secker & Warburg, 1961.

3. George Orwell, Letter to Michael Meyer, 23rd May 1946.

4. Interview with the author, 2022.

5. An azalea, planted by Orwell beneath his bedroom window, still flourished at Barnhill when I visited in the autumn of 2021.

6. *Interview with Margaret Fletcher*, Arena, BBC, 1983.

7. Stephen Wadhams, *The Orwell Tapes*, Locarno Press, 2017.

8. George Woodcock, *The Crystal Spirit: A Study of George Orwell*, Little Brown, 1966.

9. Christopher Hitchens, *Address to the Commonwealth Club, California*, 21st October 2002.

10. Alistair McKechnie and brother and sister Donald and Katie Darroch.

11. Donald Ewen Darroch, interview for Caledonia TV, 2021

12. Stephen Wadhams, *The Orwell Tapes*, Locarno Press, 2017.

13. George Orwell, Letter to George Woodcock, 2nd September 1946.

14. George Woodcock, *The Crystal Spirit: A Study of George Orwell*, Little Brown, 1966.

15. Stephen Wadhams, *The Orwell Tapes*, Locarno Press, 2017.

16. Stephen Wadhams, *The Orwell Tapes*, Locarno Press, 2017.

17. Interview with Bernard Crick, 3rd September 1976.

18. Norman Bissell, *Barnhill: A Novel*, Luath Press, 2019.

19. Thurston Clarke, *13 O'Clock*, Panther, 1984.

20. Jeffrey Meyers, *Orwell: The Wintry Conscience of a Generation*, W. W. Norton, 2000.

21. Interview with Bernard Crick, 3rd September 1976.

22. Stephen Wadhams, *The Orwell Tapes*, Locarno Press, 2017.

23. Richard Bradford, *Orwell: A Man Of Our Time*, Bloomsbury Caravel, 2020.

24. Gordon Wright, *Jura & George Orwell*, D.G.B. Wright, Isle of Jura, 1993.

25. Richard Blair, *Life With My Aunt Avril Blair*, The Orwell Society, 2011.

26. George Orwell, *Domestic Dairies*, 4th January 1947.

CHAPTER 8

1. George Orwell, *Tribune*, 14th February 1947.

2. Bernard Crick, Introduction to *The Lion and the Unicorn*, Penguin, 1982.

3. Stephen Wadhams, *The Orwell Tapes*, Locarno Press, 2017.

4. XV International brigade in Spain, https://internationalbrigades-inspain.weebly.com/scottish-volunteers.html.

5. George Orwell, *Tribune, As I Please*, 24th March 1944.

6. George Orwell, *Notes on Nationalism*, Polemic, October 1945.

7. Audrey Coppard & Bernard Crick, *Orwell Remembered*, Aerial Books/BBC, 1984.

8. Audrey Coppard & Bernard Crick, *Orwell Remembered*, Aerial Books/BBC, 1984.

9. George Orwell, *Notes on Nationalism*, Polemic, 1945.

10. The Yalta agreement of 1945 saw Germany and Europe carved up by Britain, the United States and the Soviet Union.

Endnotes

11. George Orwell, *As I Please, Tribune*, 14th February 1947.

12. Curiously, the nature-loving Orwell encountered these Scottish wild roses on Jura in late June 1946, recording in his diary: 'The common white rose of these parts is now coming into blossom. A white flower with tendency to pink at the edges … leaves have a faint sweetbriar smell'. At least Orwell's sense of smell concurs with MacDiarmid's.

13. Roland Muirhead's notes of Graham's speech at Stirling, 23rd June 1931.

14. Robert Cunninghame Graham, *The Imperial Kailyard*, 1896.

15. Robert Cunninghame Graham, *The Ipané*, Fisher, Unwin, 1899.

16. Tom Nairn, *The Break-Up of* Britain, NLB, 1977.

17. BBC *Question Time*, 13th May, 2021.

18. Richard Blair, interview for Caledonia TV, 2021.

CHAPTER 9

1. Richard Blair, interview with *Arena*, 1983 & Presentation to Orwell Society.

2. George Orwell, Letter to Sonia Brownell, 12th April 1947.

3. Jeffrey Meyers, *Orwell: The Wintry Conscience of a Generation*, W. W. Norton, 2000.

4. Audrey Coppard & Bernard Crick, *Orwell Remembered*, Aerial Books/BBC, 1984.

5. Richard Rees, *George Orwell: Fugitive from the Camp of Victory*, Secker & Warburg, 1961.

6. Stephen Wadhams, *The Orwell Tapes*, Locarno Press, 2017.

7. Stephen Wadhams, *The Orwell Tapes*, Locarno Press, 2017.

8. Blair Rozga, interview with Caledonia TV, 2021.

9. When Avril Blair left Jura, she gave members of the Rozga family one each of her brother's dining room chairs. One sits in a corner of Margaret and Blair Rozga's Islay dining room. I can never visit them without sitting on it for a few moments.

10. George Orwell, *As I Please, Tribune*, 24th January 1947.

11. *Orwell and Politics*, edited by Peter Davidson, Penguin 2001.

12. 'Dead sea fruit' is something that appears to be full of promise but is nothing but disillusion and disappointment.

13. Stephen Wadhams, *The Orwell Tapes*, Locarno Press, 2017.

14. Audrey Coppard and Bernard Crick, *Orwell Remembered*, Aerial Books/BBC, 1984.

15. Richard Blair, interview with Caledonia TV, 2021.

16. Martin Martin, *A Description of the Western Isles*, 1703.

17. Michael Powell, *A Life In Movies: An Autobiography*, Heinemann, 1986.

18. Stephen Wadhams, *The Orwell Tapes*, Locarno Press, 2017.

19. George Orwell's diary, 19th August 1947.

20. Letter to Lydia Jackson, 24th May 1948.

21. Audrey Coppard & Bernard Crick, *Orwell Remembered*, Aerial Books/BBC, 1984.

22. George Orwell, Letter to Anthony Powell, 29th November 1947.

23. Stephen Wadhams, The Orwell Tapes, Locarno Press, 2017.

24. George Orwell, Letter to Celia Kirwan, 7th December 1947.

CHAPTER 10

1. George Orwell, Letter to Tosco Fyvel, 31st December 1947.

2. George Orwell, *Towards European Unity*, Partisan Review, July/August 1947.

3. George Orwell, *You and the Atom Bomb*, *Tribune*, 19th October 1945.

4. Kenneth Roy, *The Invisible Spirit*, ICS Books, 2013.

5. While at Cranham Sanatorium in March 1949, Orwell recalled the kindness and consideration shown to him at Hairmyres but felt 'the difference in the *texture* of life when one is paying one's own keep'. The implication is that he was not a private patient at Hairmyres.

6. George Orwell, Letter to Celia Kirwan, 20th January 1948.

7. Interview with James Williamson, Arena, BBC, 1983.

8. Stephen Wadhams, *The Orwell Tapes*, Locarno Press, 2017.

9. Stephen Wadhams, *The Orwell Tapes*, Locarno Press, 2017.

Endnotes

10. That patient, Robert J. Dole, died at the age of ninety-eight in 2021. Bob Dole had been treated for infections caused by serious wounds sustained during the Second World War. He went on to become the Republican Leader of the US Senate and was the Republican presidential nominee in 1966 and vice-presidential nominee in 1976.

11. Audrey Coppard & Bernard Crick, *Orwell Remembered*, Aerial Books/BBC, 1984.

12. George Orwell's Diary, 30th March 1948.

13. George Orwell, Letter to Julian Symons, 20th April, 1948.

14. George Orwell, Letter to Roger Senhouse, 6th (?) May 1948.

15. George Orwell, Letter to Julian Symons, 10th May 1848.

16. George Orwell, Letter to Celia Kirwan, 27th May 1948.

17. Letter to David Astor, 4th May 1948.

18. Less than three weeks before Orwell's release the National Health Service had been born, with over 400 Scottish voluntary and local authority hospitals passing into state ownership and making Orwell one of the first patients to be discharged from an NHS hospital.

19. Audrey Coppard & Bernard Crick, *Orwell Remembered*, Aerial Books/BBC, 1984.

20. George Orwell, Letter to David Astor, 9th October 1948.

21. *Nineteen Eighty Four the Facsimile of the Extant Manuscript by Orwell George*, Secker & Warburg, London/M & S Press, Weston, Massachusetts, 1984.

22. George Orwell, Letter to Frederick Warburg, 22nd October 1948.

23. George Orwell, Letter to Julian Symons, 29th October 1948.

24. The Soviet Union conducted its first nuclear test ten months later, on 29th August 1949.

25. Picturesque though they are, Warburg's Jura mules were a complete invention.

26. Richard Blair, interview for Caledonia TV, 2021.

27. George Orwell, Letter to Richard Rees, 28th January 1949.

28. Orwell's notebook, 17th April 1949.

29. T.R. Fyvel, *George Orwell, A Personal Memoir*, Weidenfeld and Nicolson, 1982.

30. Richard Blair, interview for Caledonia TV, 2021.

31. Stephen Wadhams, *The Orwell Tapes*, Locarno Press, 2017.

32. Stephen Wadhams, *The Orwell Tapes*, Locarno Press, 2017.

CHAPTER 11

1. Thomas Pynchon, *Introduction to Nineteen Eighty-Four*, Penguin, 2000.

2. George Orwell, *Looking Back on the Spanish Civil War*, New Road, 1942.

3. George Orwell, *Review, The Invasion From Mars*, by Henry Cantril, New Statesman & Nation, 26th October 1940.

4. George Orwell, *Looking Back on the Spanish Civil War*, New Road, 1942.

CHAPTER 12

1. George Orwell, Note from last literary notebook, 1949.

2. Stephen Wadhams, *The Orwell Tapes*, Locarno Press, 2017.

3. Stephen Wadhams, *The Orwell Tapes*, Locarno Press, 2017.

4. *Orwell Society Journal*, No. 19, Autumn 2021.

5. Stephen Wadhams, *The Orwell Tapes*, Locarno Press, 2017.

6. Rayner Heppenstall, *The Twentieth Century*, May 1955.

7. Interview with Dr. James Williamson, *Arena*, BBC, 1983.

8. Audrey Coppard & Bernard Crick, *Orwell Remembered*, Aerial Books/BBC, 1984.

9. Timothy Garton Ash, *The File: A Personal History*, Flamingo, 1997.

10. George Orwell, *Nineteen Eighty-Four*, Secker & Warburg, 1949.

AFTERWORD

1. Anthony Powell, *George Orwell*, The Atlantic, 1967.

2. George Orwell Letter to Stephen Spender, 15th? April 1938.

3. George Orwell, *The Road to Wigan Pier*, 1937.

BIBLIOGRAPHY

4. Douglas Kerr, *Orwell & Empire*, Oxford University Press, 2022.
5. George Orwell, Letter to Francis Henson, 16th June 1949. Extracts published in *Life* and the *New York Times Book Review.*

BIBLIOGRAPHY

Timothy Garton Ash, *The File: A Personal History*, Flamingo, 1997.

Norman Bissell, *Barnhill: A Novel*, Luath Press, 2019.

Richard Bradford, *Orwell: A Man of our Time*, Bloomsbury Caravel, 2020.

Angus Calder, *Scotlands of the Mind,* Luath Press, 2002.

Thurston Clarke, *13 O'Clock*, Panther, 1984.

Audrey Coppard & Bernard Crick, *Orwell Remembered*, Aerial Books/BBC, 1984.

Bernard Crick, *Orwell: A Life*, Secker & Warburg, 1980.

Bernard Crick, Introduction to *The Lion and the Unicorn*, Penguin, 1982.

Robert Cunningham Graham, *The Imperial Kailyard*. The Twentieth Century Press Ltd, 1896.

Robert Cunninghame Graham, *The Ipané*, Fisher, Unwin, 1899.

Peter Davidson (editor), *Orwell and Politics*, Penguin, 2001.

Tom Devine, *To the Ends of the Earth*, Allan Lane, 2011.

Michael Fry, *The Scottish Empire*, The Tuckwell Press & Birlinn, 2001.

Tosco Fyvel: *George Orwell: A Life*, Weidenfeld & Nicolson, 1982.

Catherine Hall, Nicolas Draper, Keith McClelland, Kate Donington, and Rachael Lang, *Legacies of British Slave-Ownership: Colonial Slavery and the Formation of Victorian Britain,* Cambridge University Press, 2014.

Rosina Harrison, *Rose: My Life in Service*, Cassell, 1976.

Christopher Hitchens, Address to the Commonwealth Club, California, 21st October 2002. YouTube.

Book title

Christopher Hitchens, *Why Orwell Matters*, Basic Books, 2002.

James K. Hopkins, *Into the Heart of the Fire: The British in the Spanish Civil War*, Stanford University Press, 1996.

Douglas Kerr, *Orwell & Empire*, Oxford University Press, 2022.

Captain J. Lawrence-Archer, *Monumental Inscriptions of the British West Indies*, 1875.

Edward Long, *The History of Jamaica*,1774.

Dorian Lynskey, *The Ministry of Truth, A Biography of George Orwell's 1944*, Picador, 2019.

Allister MacMillan, *Seaports of the Far East*, 1925.

Alex Massie, introduction to 'Jura edition' of *Nineteen Eighty-Four*, Birlinn, 2021.

Jeffrey Meyers, *Orwell: The Wintry Conscience of a Generation*, W. W. Norton, 2000.

Tom Nairn, *The Break-Up of* Britain, NLB, 1977.

Peter Obourn, *The Assault on Truth,* Simon & Schuster, 2021.

George Orwell, *A Clergyman's Daughter*, Victor Gollancz, 1935.

George Orwell, *The Road to Wigan Pier*, Victor Gollancz,1937.

George Orwell, *Homage to Catalonia,* Secker & Warburg, 1938.

George Orwell, *Coming Up For Air*, Victor Gollancz, 1939.

George Orwell, *Animal Farm*, Secker & Warburg, 1945.

George Orwell, *Nineteen Eighty-Four*, Secker & Warburg, 1949.

George Orwell, *Collected Essays, Journalism and Letters*, Penguin, 1970.

George Orwell, *Nineteen Eighty-Four: The Facsimile of the Extant Manuscript*, Secker & Warburg/M & S Press, Weston, Massachusetts, 1984.

Michael Powell, *A Life in Movies*, Heinemann, 1986.

Thomas Pynchon, *Introduction to Nineteen Eighty-Four*, Penguin, 2000.

Richard Rees, *George Orwell: Fugitive from the Camp of Victory*, Secker & Warburg, 1961.

Kenneth Roy, *The Invisible Spirit*, ICS Books, 2013.

ACKNOWLEDGEMENTS

Rebecca Solnit, *Orwell's Roses*, Granta, 2021.

Peter Stansky and William Abrahams, *The Unknown Orwell*, Constable, 1972.

Jonathan Swift, *The Publick Spirit of the Whigs*, 1714.

D.J. Taylor, *Orwell: The New Life*, Constable, 2023.

Edward M. Thomas, *Orwell*, Writers & Critics series, Oliver & Boyd, 1965.

Sylvia Topp, *Eileen: The Making of George Orwell*, Unbound, 2020.

University College London, Center for the Study of the Legacies of British Slavery, Database, 2020.

Stephen Wadhams, *The Orwell Tapes*, Locarno Press, 2017.

Frederic Warburg, *All Authors Are Equal*, Hutchison, 1973.

Les Wilson, *Putting the Tea in Britain: How Scots Made Our National Drink*, Birlinn, 2021.

George Woodcock, *The Crystal Spirit: A Study of George Orwell*, Little Brown, 1966.

Gordon Wright, *Jura & George Orwell*, D.G.B. Wright, Isle of Jura, 1993.

XV International Brigade in Spain, https://internationalbrigadesin-spain.weebly.com/scottish-volunteers.html.

ACKNOWLEDGEMENTS

Everyone who writes about Orwell today does so in the illuminating bright light of the twenty-volume *Complete Works of George Orwell*, edited by Peter Davison and published by Secker & Warburg in 1998. Sadly, Peter died 2022 and I never had the privilege of meeting him and thanking him for his magisterial collection and painstaking scholarship. I have also delved into the works of scores of other scholars and writers whose biographies, autobiographies and memoirs have informed this book. My heartfelt thanks to them all, some of whose well-thumbed works have long been on my bookshelves. While these authors are recorded in the footnotes of *Orwell's Island*, there are other people who deserve their contributions being recognised.

Much of my early research was done for the documentary *Sàr-Sgeòil: Nineteen Eighty-Four* directed by myself, produced by Julie McCrone and presented by Cathy MacDonald for BBC ALBA and first transmitted in December 2021. Julie and Cathy could not have been better colleagues and their dedication and inspiration spilled over from the TV production and into my book. Mary Ann MacDonald of Berneray, North Uist, translated Oceana's three chilling slogans into Gaelic for that documentary, and I have recycled them in this book. *Mòran taing.* Many thanks too to Margaret Mary Murray of BBC ALBA for her continuing support of our bookish series *Sàr-Sgeòil* (Classic Tales) and of the Orwell programme in particular.

My thanks also to those who generously gave of their time and memories as interviewees for our documentary, and who I have quoted throughout the book – in particular Richard Blair, formerly of Barnhill on the island of Jura and champion of both his father's work and the educational initiatives of the Orwell Society. The interview Richard gave us for the documentary was outstanding, and I have filleted it ruthlessly for this book. Thank you too, Richard, for permission to use family photographs from the Jura years. My other invaluable living link to George Orwell – or 'Mr. Blair' as she always knew him – is Fiona Fletcher C.V.O., the oldest child of Margaret and Robin Fletcher who owned the Ardlussa Estate on Jura when Orwell lived there. With wit and gusto Fiona shared with me her vivid memories of the writer during his Jura days.

Donald Ewen Darroch of Jura, and Blair Rozga of Islay also revealed their Orwell lore – fascinating memories passed down by parents who got to know Eric and Avril well.

Damaris Fletcher has been a stalwart of my Fletcher family

ACKNOWLEDGEMENTS

fact-checking (any mistakes are mine, not hers). Thanks also to Sophie Allsopp, Damaris's daughter-in-law, who transported myself, my filming colleagues and our equipment over the last rough miles to Barnhill and graciously showed us Orwell's writing room where I stood in reverence.

I am in debt to poet and academic Dr Peter Mackay, of St Andrews University, for revealing to me the marvellous metaphor that the publicly owned River Orwell is for Orwell's political ideals. He and writer Màiri Kidd's opinions sharpened my own insights into Orwell's Scotophobia and the benign influence that Jura had on him. Orwell was indeed 'A man arguing all the time with his own prejudices and his own fears, his own bigotries, his own shortcomings …' as Christopher Hitchens so astutely pointed out. My thanks too to the inspiring 'Hitch', sadly missed but fondly recalled. I cherish the memories of working on a documentary with him and our 'Orwellian' conversations over drinks and dinner when filming was done for the day. Most of these were in the company of Tom Nairn, whose role in shaping a very different Scottish Nationalism to the one that Orwell feared is immeasurable. Sadly, Tom passed away as I completed this book.

The Orwell Society Journal has been a rich source of leads, information and inspiration. My sincere thanks and best wishes for many editions still to come and to its editor, Masha Karp, staff and contributors.

Gràcies to independent Orwell scholar Darcy Moore whose tweets are always illuminating, especially the one alerting me to the existence of *The Spanish Revolution, Bulletin of the Worker's Party of Marxist Unification P.O.U.M.*, from February 1937.

The staff of the National Museum of Scotland were (again) their marvelously efficient and helpful selves. Stepping into the George IV Bridge entrance is a liminal experience – you may emerge profoundly changed.

ORWELL'S ISLAND

Sara Hunt at Saraband first saw potential in *Orwell's Island* and, along with her colleague Rosie Hilton and inspirational editor Craig Hillsley, cranked up my determination to hone the final text to a level beyond my initial ambition. Thank you all, as well as to Ellie Croston and to Ellie Johnson for proofreading.

I am grateful for permission to quote from the following:

'Ballad of the Taxi Driver's Cap', © Hamish Henderson, from *Ballads of World War II*, Hamish Henderson, 1947: permission granted courtesy of the Literary Estate of Hamish Henderson, and in particular, Janet Henderson.

'The Little White Rose of Scotland', 1931, © Hugh MacDiarmid, from *Complete Poems Vol I*, ed. Michael Grieve and W.R. Aitken (paperback, 2017), Carcanet Press, Manchester.

Caledonia: A Fragment, © Anthony Powell, privately printed, permission granted courtesy of David Higham Associates.

Last, but not least, my heartfelt thanks to my remarkable wife Jenni Minto for putting up with my silences and absences (often more mental than physical) as I shared two years of my life with my near neighbour over on Jura, the great George Orwell.

INDEX

INDEX

A former political journalist, **Les Wilson** is an award-winning writer and documentary maker. His films have revealed the lives of Robert Burns, Thomas Telford, the 'lighthouse' Stevenson family, writer and politician Robert Cunninghame Graham and 'the father of Australia' Lachlan Macquarie. He has twice been shortlisted for the prestigious Saltire Society History Book of the Year Award at Scotland's National Book Awards, winning it in 2018 for *The Drowned and the Saved: How War Came to the Hebrides.* He is a lifelong admirer of Orwell, a member of the Orwell Society and lives on the island of Islay, Jura's neighbour.